THE BEACH PLUM INN COOKBOOK

Books by Theresa A. Morse:

LIFE IS FOR LIVING
THE BEST I EVER TASTED
NEVER IN THE KITCHEN WHEN COMPANY ARRIVES
FUTURE À LA CARTE

the Beach Plum Inn cookbook

Theresa A. Morse and Fred Feiner

DOUBLEDAY & COMPANY, INC.
Garden City, New York   1977

Drawings by Grambs Miller

ISBN: 0-385-12591-7
Library of Congress Catalog Card Number 76–42377

In Loving Memory of Warren Morse,
Founder of Beach Plum Inn

Contents

AUTHORS' NOTE

The recipes in this book have been carefully adapted for use in your kitchen and are designed in most cases to serve six.

Recipes for ingredients printed in capital letters may be found by consulting the Index.

instant innkeeping

Beach Plum Inn provides different things for different people. For some a new romance, a memorable interlude, a honeymoon, or an escape hatch from children. For others just plain fun in the sun, good company, and uniquely delicious food.

Sophisticated city dwellers find themselves embarking on extraordinary, almost embarrassing adventures. "Can this be really I?" they wonder, absorbed in digging clams, collecting wildflowers across the moors, picking blueberries and beach plums along the roadside, or walking the beaches in search of stones, shells and driftwood. Plus such conventional sports as tennis, golf, fishing, sailing, and swimming, tossed in for good measure.

Sturdily built in 1899, the inn stands on top of a hill in Menemsha on the island of Martha's Vineyard, overlooking the bright blue Sound and the Elizabeth Islands to the north and the sparkling harbor, flanked by Gay Head to the west.

It wasn't always an inn. Until a raging gale and blizzard swept over the island one cold November night in 1898, it was just a beautiful hilltop owned by a man named Ira Davis.

The storm demolished a fleet of approximately fifty schooners struggling to reach a safe berth in the Vineyard Haven harbor. The ships were smashed and their cargoes, chiefly lumber, were hurled into the sea, thrown up on Vineyard beaches, or sank out of sight. The fury of the gale drove one schooner through the dock with such force that it stuck out on both sides.

In those days salvage laws were extremely liberal. Not only was a man who saved either a ship or part of its cargo entitled to charge a percentage of the value for himself, but the courts were most supportive in effecting generous settlements. As for cash purchasers of these damaged goods—they were at a premium and were offered most enticing bargains.

According to his middle son, Arthur Davis, this bargain lumber proved irresistible to his father, who immediately decided that this was the time to build a homestead on that hilltop in Menemsha. Just big enough to house himself, his wife, and their three sons. A four-bedroom, one-and-a-half-bathroom house with, according to Arthur, "Mother's and Father's bedroom conveniently located on the ground floor opening onto the front hall, the living room, and the kitchen, so that Mother, in seconds, could jump out at us, no matter where the fight was taking place."

Eventually Arthur inherited the house and the eight acres on which it stood. But by that time he was Judge Arthur Davis, living in a beautiful home in Edgartown, which his wife had no intention of leaving, not even for a summer, in the old, rundown homestead.

Torn between practical New England thrift and an aching nostalgia, from time to time Judge Davis would decide to sell the old place—house, land and furnishings—only to snatch it back at the first sign of an interested nibble. Finally, by way of compromise, for many years he rented the house to summer visitors.

This is where matters stood, when, one June morning in 1934, my husband and I received an unexpected invitation. We were living on Long Island at the time and the letter came from a couple

INSTANT INNKEEPING

who were neighbors. The preceding summer they and their children had mysteriously disappeared. On their return in the fall they had been vague about their whereabouts, and we weren't too curious, for ours was a casual relationship. But now they wanted us to visit them on an island called Martha's Vineyard somewhere in Massachusetts about eighty miles from Boston. My Boston-born husband had never even heard of it.

To this day I don't know how they happened to invite us, and they certainly lived to regret it. But since we liked them both, were now intrigued by the mystery of their absence and since my parents-in-law owned a summer home on the ocean near Swampscott and were overjoyed at the prospect of entertaining their two young granddaughters without benefit of interfering parents, we accepted with alacrity. All set for a five-day visit to Martha's Vineyard over the Fourth of July.

Five days of sheer enchantment! Such a glorious montage of surf and sound; of picnics and cookouts; of walking the unfenced moors; of dashing into any body of water without clothes; of bright, clever people who "did things," on a grandiose scale in New York but made relaxed, amusing playmates on the Vineyard; of cocktails with more of same—writers, painters, editors, sculptors, publishers; of wearing old slacks for all occasions; of kerosene lamps and stoves and ice melting in the wooden icebox; of lobsters at a quarter apiece, regardless of weight; of digging clams before breakfast, the fragrant air, the sturdy independent islanders . . .

We loved every minute of it. All too soon we stood on the wharf watching the approaching steamer that would carry us away. Inarticulate with gratitude, we tried to express what this holiday had meant to us. Our hostess came to the rescue.

"If you really mean everything you've been saying," she said, "I'll tell you how you can best thank us. By not telling your friends back home about the Vineyard. After all, it's perfect now, but if hordes of people hear about it and start coming, it will be spoiled. If you find that you must talk about it, don't forget to mention such items as low-slung fogs, wood ticks and poison ivy."

Lucky us, how had we ever managed to break into this Utopia? We promised faithfully to keep it all a secret but there are probably a thousand people on this island today, mute testimony to the fact that we broke our promise, over and over again. There was no way of containing the joy we found on the Vineyard.

The following summer we rented The Lobster Pot, a small cottage in Menemsha which continually overflowed with family and friends who, in turn, put down sturdy Vineyard roots of their own. Weekends my husband commuted from New York, first by overnight steamer (with change at New Bedford) and then by train with long summer vacations in the middle.

The blow fell in 1944. Until then we had happily renewed our lease on The Lobster Pot before leaving for home (three hundred dollars per summer no matter how early we arrived or how late we stayed). Our schoolteacher landlady much preferred junketing around the country by automobile to settling down on the Vineyard for her summer holidays and had promised us that the cottage would be ours practically in perpetuity. Now, thanks to wartime restrictions and shortages, she could no longer travel and therefore would be occupying The Lobster Pot herself for the summer of '44.

"No one's ever going to do this to us again," raged my husband, especially angry because she had let us know at the last minute. "We're going to buy a house and have a place of our own on the Vineyard for the rest of our lives."

That summer our two daughters were slaving to feed the nation on farm camps so we rented a small cottage with another couple for a few weeks and, immediately on arrival, arranged to go house hunting with Hope Flanders, the up-island realtor. This time with intent to buy.

The fourth house that she proposed showing us was the somewhat dilapidated Davis house. We suggested skipping it because we remembered it when Judge Jerome Frank had been its summer tenant. Tiny rooms on the ground floor; the house so surrounded by trees that no view of the water existed except, so they claimed, from an upstairs window; an old-fashioned kitchen with sloping floor, zinc sink, and coal stove—she must have something better to show us.

Mrs. Flanders was insistent, offering such irrefutable arguments as the fact that we'd never seen the upstairs rooms; that it was really one of her nicest houses; and, besides, it was right on our way. Reluctantly we agreed to dash through it.

At that time a driveway ran around the house so close to the front door that it was possible to step from car to porch without touching the ground. Mrs. Flanders excused herself to go in ahead and obtain permission from the summer tenant to show the house. Sitting in the car only a few feet away, we could hear every word.

Mrs. Flanders: "May I show the house, Mrs. King?"

Mrs. King: "No need to—we're going to rent it again next summer."

Mrs. Flanders: "This isn't for renting. Judge Davis has decided to sell the house."

Mrs. King: "But you never told us!"

Mrs. Flanders: "The house only came on the market yesterday. If the Morses don't buy it, are you interested?"

Mrs. King: "Very much so."

Realtors please note. There is no finer way of bringing a client to heel. If we didn't grab this marvelous house, we knew who would. So we hurried through it paying little or no attention to such incidentals as plumbing, roof, closet space, and the like in our haste not to let it get away from us. Once outside, we urged Mrs. Flanders to take us to the owner at once.

"You're *sure?*" she asked incredulously. "I have several more houses to show you."

We were sure.

En route to Edgartown, sitting together on the back seat, we held a summit meeting. We had previously decided on what we could afford to pay for a house. Judge Davis was asking a thousand dollars more. For the furnished house and the eight acres on which it stood.

"That's called the 'asking price,'" my knowledgeable husband explained to me. "No one ever expects to get it. He'll come down."

I was dubious, feeling certain that Vineyarders would not stoop to such low tactics.

"What do you think, Mrs. Flanders?" Warren asked, leaning forward. "Is it all right if we offer Judge Davis less?" Mrs. Flanders said that it would be all right.

Judge Davis was in his office and we were shown in at once. After introductions, he and Mrs. Flanders embarked on a courtesy conversation seemingly designed to drive us out of our minds. Certainly it gave promise of lasting forever as they politely inquired after each other's family, exchanged news on up-island versus down-island fishing, and dealt leisurely with other local items. Finally our turn came.

"Well, Judge Davis," Mrs. Flanders began at long last, "the Morses are interested in buying your Menemsha house."

"Are they indeed?" The genial judge now peered at us with something resembling hostility.

My husband spoke up. "Very much so," he said, "but it's a little more than we can afford."

"Is that so?" A kindly note had crept into Judge Davis's voice. "What exactly did you expect to pay?"

Barely concealing his pleasure at the turn this conversation was taking, Warren answered, "One thousand dollars less."

Judge Davis beamed, he oozed charm. "I'm sure you can find a very nice house for that sum," he said graciously. Then, turning to Mrs. Flanders, "If the Morses don't buy my house, please remove it from the market."

The Morses bought it.

During the following winter Reginald Norton remodeled the entire house. The three little downstairs rooms were transformed into one big, comfortable living room; windows blossomed where none had been before; the kitchen floor was leveled, the kitchen modernized; floors were varnished, walls papered, and enough trees cut down to give a sweeping view of sea and sunsets.

The summer of '45 was our first in the new home, which, until 1952, housed a steady stream of friends and relatives, a new son-in-law, kindness of our daughter Jean, then two grandchildren, Wendy and Warren. During this time we bought an army barracks, moved it from Peaked Hill to our land, where Roger Engley turned it into a charming two-bedroom cottage to accommodate our overflow.

By 1950 we were more in love with the Vineyard and less enchanted with life in New York than ever before. For the next two years we flirted with the highly desirable, totally impractical, idea of moving to the Vineyard for keeps and living happily ever after. By that time Jean and Ernie were settled in Cleveland; Carol, our younger daughter, was beginning a career with Young Audiences; and we could do pretty much as we pleased.

Over and over again we weighed the pros and cons of such a move. If we stayed in New York we could count on a comfortable income, good friends, time to travel each winter and a Vineyard holiday each summer. Not such a horrible prospect. On the minus side were the long hours and tensions inherent in my husband's business, high blood pressure for him, and a strong, unshakable feeling on both our parts that something vital and challenging was missing in our lives. Would we continue on this somewhat breathless and altogether predictable merry-go-round for the rest of our days, or was there something important that we were missing?

We backed and filled, blew hot and cold, were enthusiastic one minute, scared stiff the next. In the year 1952 it was not exactly fashionable for sane and sensible people to kick over the traces and start over again for no good reason. And although we had enough money to keep the wolf from howling at the door in the immediate future, nevertheless we would need to be gainfully employed if that pleasant condition were to last.

When we turned our attention to just how we could live on the Vineyard and be gainfully employed, our choices were limited. No one needed a textile broker on the island nor a professional fund raiser. Warren made a very fine martini but Menemsha has always been dry. I was a pretty good cook but neither willing nor able to make a career of it. Or so I thought.

Some people collect paintings, rare books, or even piggy banks. We, through the years, had collected small, informal inns, preferably with owner-hosts and dedicated to the purpose of making guests welcome, comfortable, and extremely well fed.

Such places are rare which made our collection that much more valuable. We found some of our best in Bantam, Connecticut, in St. Thomas, V.I., and in Taormina, Sicily. It took only a little more frenzied living, a slightly higher blood pressure, and suddenly we were talking about turning our Vineyard home into Beach Plum Inn. Finally, against the advice of caring friends and relatives (did we know what it was like to plummet from a "have" to a "have-not"?) we settled our affairs in New York, sent out seventy-five sea-blue announcements of the coming opening of Beach Plum Inn, and moved, lock, stock, and many barrels, to Martha's Vineyard.

That first summer was a cross between a nightmare and a festival. "Nightmare" because we really didn't know what we were doing or how to do it. "Festival" because we so hugely enjoyed it, in spite of working harder than ever before. We met all guests at the ferry (a round trip of twenty-two miles), escorted them to flower-filled rooms, carefully recorded their food preferences and idiosyncrasies, served breakfast to fishing folk at six in the morning, met planes at midnight, seldom sat down, but had a wonderful time.

Hilda, our maid in New York, came along as cook, and we ran the inn pretty much as we'd run our home, which didn't add up to a very handsome profit. At the end of that first summer we had netted a sickly $950, although Warren insisted, comfortingly, that many businesses lose money, lots of it, the first year.

Some mistakes we weren't likely to make again. Such as renting an outside room for occasional overflow guests and reducing the rates we charged those good sports who were willing to bed down away from us. Rates that first year were twelve dollars per day, per person, and this included three hearty meals. Our benighted reasoning for the reduction went as follows: Presumably guests in an outside room would be less comfortable, less cosseted, than under our roof. So we charged them ten dollars apiece and paid their landlady four dollars per day. This is not the road to riches.

At the end of the second season we found a new road, perhaps it could more accurately be called a lane. So many people asked me so many questions such as, "How do you like having your husband around the house all day?" "What's it like to run a small inn?" etc., that I wrote a book called *Future à la Carte*, which was published in 1955. While sales did not exactly skyrocket, nevertheless five thousand lovely people bought it.

Our third season was a beauty. We had hit our stride, knew what we were doing. The inn could now accommodate twelve guests and on that balmy evening of August 10, my birthday, we were awash with euphoria. Dinner was over, an especially splendid one, and now lighted lanterns swung from the trees while guests sat drinking coffee at small tables surrounding a fragrant, old-fashioned garden in front. From the house where Warren sat at the piano came the lilting strains of Gershwin and Porter.

Suddenly the telephone rang and our lives were never again quite the same. We could hear it clearly from the garden, but no one summoned me, and it was a few minutes before a frantic Hilda beckoned me into the house.

The phone call had been for her. It came from a member of Alcoholics Anonymous, an organization in which Paul, her husband, was an outstanding member, so good that he was often sent to prisons and factories to lecture and help others. His record had been uniquely excellent until the night before when he had suffered a "slip"—a euphemism for a blockbuster of a drinking spree. Would she come home at once? Two hours later we put her on a plane for New York.

Within seconds I was demoted from hostess, companion, and shopper, to head cook, and I was anything but qualified. When I claimed earlier in these pages that I was a "pretty good cook," that was a slight exaggeration. Before I became an innkeeper's wife, our meals were considered very good but, for the most part, I planned and ordered but did not execute. Now I found myself cooking meals for twelve guests, ourselves, and four in help. Three times a day!

How often I was reminded of a long-ago incident during my childhood. My mother had advertised for a cook and the house overflowed with eager applicants. Mother sat in the library briskly interviewing the ladies, one at a time. The dialogue with the fourth ran as follows:

Mother: "Can you bake well?"
Cook: "Only fair, ma'am."
Mother: "Do you make a good gravy?"
Cook: "Just so-so."
Mother: "How about your salad dressings?"
Cook: "Mine are nothing special."
Mother (fascinated): "What wages are you asking?"
Cook: "Fifteen dollars a week." (This was top pay for those days and mother could not resist one last question.)
Mother: "Considering how little you seem to know, don't you think you're asking pretty high wages?"
Cook: "No, ma'am, I don't. It's *much* harder when you don't know how."

I learned that truer words were never spoken. The next few

days were non-stop. Daytimes I hung over the stove, barely finishing one meal before the next loomed up while Warren did the pleasant, relaxed work out front. After dinner, he played the piano and enjoyed the guests while I retired to our room to bone up on tomorrow's meals.

A reprieve from prison sentence, a legacy when facing starvation, are trifles compared to my relief when Hilda finally telephoned. Paul had been sent to a "drying-out station" for the next three weeks. Did I want her back? DID I?

But I had learned my lesson. Never again would I find myself in this uncomfortable predicament. Never again would we serve a dish that I could not make. As soon as the inn closed that summer, we began casting about for a school for me.

The London Cordon Bleu Cookery School not only offered everything we were seeking but had the added charm of being in London. Off went my dossier, such as it was, to Muriel Downes and Rosemary Hume, the two heads. To my astonished delight, I was accepted. I suspect that my frantic need must have seeped through to them.

I loved every minute of it. Miss Downes and Miss Hume are superb teachers, in love with their craft and eager to share this joy with their pupils. Strict, all-seeing, maintaining the highest standards—these ladies have turned out a good many fine cooks from many countries.

Beach Plum Inn, under our aegis, lasted for seventeen years. While we never had room for more than twelve guests, gradually we began booking outsiders for dinner on the porch overlooking the sea and soon we were serving a maximum of thirty-four each evening. That is, each evening when the weather was mild and pleasant. When taking reservations we also requested telephone numbers and should there be rain or cold, we were forced to cancel outsiders. Looking back, I marvel at their good nature.

Once again, people began asking questions, this time about food. How did we make that cucumber soup, that chocolate torte, that baked stuffed lamb? The end result of this was a cookbook called *Never in the Kitchen When Company Arrives,* published by Doubleday and designed for the hostess-cook who does *everything*. All menus designed for six. This was published simultane-

INSTANT INNKEEPING

ously in England with a prized foreword by Muriel Downes. It was followed, a few years later, by *The Best I Ever Tasted.*

The years raced by. We worked very hard spring, summer, and fall, but the winters belonged to us and we made the most of them. New countries, new languages, new recipes . . . During this time Carol, our younger daughter, after ten years as National Executive Director of Young Audiences and to the overwhelming relief of her mother (who, she claims, was indecently joyful) married Fred Feiner. Joyful we were! First, because we liked Fred and second, because we had found marriage to be a very fine institution.

So there they were in New York—Fred an executive in a national discount chain and Carol still heading up Young Audiences. Along came Jimmy, just what everybody wanted. We all knew where we were heading.

Or so we thought until Carol and Fred began making casual remarks and tentative suggestions that we didn't take too seriously. Such as, "Do you ever think about selling the inn—you've run it for a long time?" or "If you ever do decide to sell the inn, will you give us the refusal?"

Occasionally we discussed this possibility by ourselves and agreed that two unlikelier innkeepers couldn't be found. Both were geared to New York living, neither knew much about food or cooking, and although Carol had enjoyed a brief experience as assistant manager in an upstate New York inn and Fred firmly believed that if you can run a business, you can run an inn, we weren't sure that this was so.

But they persisted. Gently and with logic they managed to convince us that not only could they do it, but that it was to the interests of all concerned that they do it soon. No one, least of all us, was getting any younger. They could hire a Cordon Bleu cook and thus maintain standards. We could help launch them; it was now or never. Suddenly it seemed like a fine idea and we were consulting lawyers.

The inn changed hands legally on January 28, 1969, just a few days after Warren died. We were en route for a winter vacation in the south and, as though his time had run out, he peacefully and quietly stopped breathing. Thus it was I, alone, who helped the

Feiners through the transition and they, in turn, helped me to find myself and a new life.

That spring the place was filled with workmen as carefully designed blueprints became stunning realities. A new dining room overlooking the harbor, two terrace rooms, each with private bath, an enlarged garden, increased parking space, new quarters for the help seemed to spring up overnight. And so, in June 1969, the Feiners opened for their first season as owners of Beach Plum Inn.

It took three summers for them to find their inn legs so to speak. So many problems, so much to do in such a short time. Their basic goals matched ours all the way—to give their guests cosseting, fun, and the best possible food. They reversed our roles in that Carol became the front man in charge of bookings, reservations and staff, while Fred was responsible for the kitchen.

My one concern was the food. It was excellent but totally dependent on the cook. Even though Fred had taken some courses in cooking at Northeastern University, he was by no means qualified to handle the cooking alone. If anything happened to the cook . . .

Right after the third season I began to nag.

"I'd certainly hate to be in your shoes," I said to Fred one fine day when we were lunching alone.

"What does that mean?"

"It means that I'd hate owning an inn in which my cook knew more than I did."

"So what are you suggesting?"

"Look, Fred," I said gently, wishing I'd never started this, "you know a lot more than when you started and I know you've taken some courses. But three months at the London Cordon Bleu would make you an expert. . . ."

Fred bellowed. Not a chance. He wasn't going to leave Carol and Jimmy for three months.

I reminded him of the Hilda debacle and finally made him an offer.

"Think it over," I said. "If you do go, I'll take care of Jimmy for three weeks in the middle and Carol can go to London and have a holiday with you."

That did it.

Next problem—getting him into the course. Fortunately

Muriel Downes, on a lecture tour in this country, spent a weekend with me.

"He doesn't qualify for this course," she told me regretfully when I explained the situation.

"Maybe not in experience or basic training but he's a hard worker, deeply interested. . . ."

"But we could never give him a diploma."

"He doesn't care."

"Nor a recommendation."

"He won't be looking to you for a job."

"All right," she said, "but remember—no diploma."

The rest is family history. Fred found the going rough at first. The French bothered him, the British English was foreign to his ears. Teachers talked fast and furiously, demonstrations moved at a headlong pace. It took a few weeks before he found himself, but when he did, there was no holding him. Three months later he returned from England proudly carrying a diploma from the London Cordon Bleu Cookery School.

Fred has become an exceptional cook. He is imaginative and inventive and, best of all, his recipes are easy to follow. The ever-ringing telephone at Beach Plum Inn is testimony to the excellence of the food and this is due entirely to Fred.

Once again guests are begging for recipes. Could we have the recipe for Bombe Favorite, for lemon soup, for striped bass with lobster sauce, and for dozens of others. This book is the answer. And because I have stayed close to Beach Plum Inn throughout the years and because Fred and I have studied and experimented together, this book is a collaboration and includes what we consider our best and most popular recipes. They have been tailored for home entertaining and, for the most part, are designed to serve six. The exceptions are those entrees where leftovers would make another delicious meal. We hope this book will give you some new ideas, new recipes, and the stimulus that a new cookbook gives those of us who love cooking.

THERESA A. MORSE

THE BEACH PLUM INN COOKBOOK

kitchen maneuvers

If you will think of the kitchen as a combination workshop and bank, you will have a lot going for you. Such as the incentive to prepare delicious food and the ability to do it in the least possible time.

First the workshop. You have probably been cooking long enough to have amassed the tools and equipment that mean the most to you. Each of us has her own ideas of comfort and efficiency in the kitchen. Some of us dote on open peg boards crammed with such essential items as strainers, whips, tongs, graters, trivets, and copper pans. Others want everything out of sight. Some treasure large, permanent chopping boards, others prefer small, portable ones. Be that as it may, there are a few special kitchen tools which not only make for speed and efficiency but without which, in our judgment, no kitchen is complete.

Our number one choice is the blender. If you haven't got one, beg, nag, or slave for it. It not only takes the drudgery out of endless small jobs but turns out wonderful food as well. In record time the versatile blender will chop nuts, grind bread or cracker crumbs, purée vegetables, chop parsley, cream spinach, make mayonnaise, Hollandaise sauce, French dressing, and much more besides (see any blender recipe book). We hear some undeserved complaints about cleaning this magical equipment. All you need to do is squirt some liquid soap into the jar, half-fill with water, put on the lid, and press any button you choose. Presto!—in seconds it is clean.

Mixers are nice to own but not essential. An egg beater or small electric hand-mixer will do most jobs just as well unless you are a homemade bread buff or do a lot of baking. What you really don't need is a flour sifter unless you happen to own one which, oddly enough, practically everyone does. They are limited as to use —after all, what can they do except sift flour or sugar, whereas a strainer will do just as good a job and dozens of others besides. With a strainer you can sift flour and sugar to perfection but you can also use it to wash and drain fruits and vegetables or the contents of a can, you can strain soups, applesauce, or cooked vegetables. For added charms—they are inexpensive, easy to wash, and hang gracefully and conveniently on the peg board.

If you have never owned an enamel double boiler, you will be amazed at how often you use it. Wonderful for sauces, melting chocolate, anything involving eggs as opposed to aluminum which tends to discolor them. It is also easy to clean.

Wire or balloon whisks in several sizes are a boon. They blend, mix, and incorporate almost anything. Equally valuable are rubber scrapers in different sizes (how did our grandmothers ever get along without them?). And if you haven't a vegetable peeler— run, don't walk. . . .

You can make your own cutters for toast rounds, cookies, tarts, and all else calling for cutters. Take a small can (tomato paste), a medium-sized can (tomato soup) and a large can (tomatoes) and remove both the top and the bottom of each can. Wash well, remove labels, and nest. The advantage of the open-end cans is that you can make a dozen or so rounds at a time and push them through and out.

We come now to recipes. We keep them in two boxes and hope you'll do the same. One contains the tried and true, the other those that you have begged, stolen, or copied from books and magazines but never gotten around to trying. Make them earn their way into the master file. That beautiful dessert recipe that you coaxed from a reluctant hostess might be missing an ingredient or two. You have to find out.

When it comes to tackling a recipe, new or old, you can save yourself a lot of misery by reading it all the way through, then assembling all the ingredients before going to work. For sheer frustration, discovering halfway through that a vital ingredient is missing can't be beat.

This seems as good a place as any to mention the charms of cleaning as you go—an act which requires stamina but is deliciously rewarding. That is, unless you happen to have a helpmate who is touched by the sight of your sink full of dirty dishes and, reliably, springs to the rescue. Most unusual.

The refrigerator makes a dandy bank. The bottom is your kitchen checking account, the freezer top your savings. If you own a big freezer, so much the better, but you can perform miracles with only the freezer section of your refrigerator.

For the refrigerator checking account, we recommend depositing:

A small jar of fresh lemon juice. Fresh lemon juice adds zest and flavor to salad dressings, vegetables, sauces, and some fruits.

Homemade mayonnaise. For sheer deliciousness, no commercial brand comes close. With a pinch of curry or a little extra lemon juice, it enhances everything it touches from chicken sandwiches to beautiful salads (see Index).

Miscellaneous items. Half a pint of sour cream, a bag of carrots, celery, a jar of grated cheese (use up your leftover hard cheese), fresh green peppers, a jar of capers, and fresh mushrooms. If mushrooms are snowy white when you buy them and immediately poured into a plastic bag, tightly tied, and stored in the salad compartment, they will keep for at least a week.

We come now to the freezer savings account. When freezers

first came on the market, delighted housewives would load them with ice cream and bread (two items easily purchased at nearby stores). Now we put them to real use. Apart from storing home-made cakes, pies, rolls, desserts of all kinds, canapés, meat, cooked vegetables, etc., they contain aids to cooking that can be lifesavers on a busy day.

Take chopped onions, for example. Recipes calling for them are a great nuisance at times. What could be nicer than taking a frosty ball out of the freezer and paring the needed amount right into the skillet? You can keep ahead by finely chopping half a dozen onions on a non-busy day, spooning them into a freezer bag, and stashing them away. True, you can buy these already chopped and frozen but they cost considerably more and deprive you of that lovely do-it-yourself satisfaction. Besides, the tears are good for your eyes.

The same goes for chopped nuts. Very convenient on a busy morning to pour the needed amount out of a freezer bag. They also require no defrosting and keep almost indefinitely. Beside, nuts are a bargain at Christmastime when the supermarkets sell them in larger-than-usual quantities for less money. If you really want to save—buy nuts in the shell and put the whole family to work cracking them open.

Egg whites freeze beautifully and can be stored in jars, labeled as to contents and number, ready for making meringues, cookies, glazing, and many desserts. We always manage to freeze one by it-self to use as that extra egg white that makes a soufflé reach for the sky. Yolks can be frozen, too, covered with water, but we don't recommend it. They never seem totally intact on emerging. In-stead, if we have several, we make Hollandaise sauce in the blender. That freezes very well and, after defrosting, can be heated by placing the jar in hot, not boiling, water. If it's a matter of one or two yolks—drop them gently into boiling water and let them hard-cook. Grated over the salad bowl or vegetables, such as broccoli, spinach, or asparagus, they add glamour and interest.

Stock in the freezer is real treasure. Perhaps it comes from boiling chickens to use in salad, sandwiches, crepes, etc., perhaps from the pan in which steak or hamburgers were broiled or from your roasting pan. Add water to any such pan, bring to a boil on top of the stove, and scrape the flavorful particles into the liquid. Strained, seasoned to taste, and given time for the fat to rise to the top and be removed, such stock, frozen, will be conveniently on hand as the base or to flavor soups, gravies, and vegetable dishes.

Whipped cream stored in the freezer is a security blanket. Here's how it works. When entertaining guests for dinner, buy a half pint of heavy cream to serve with the coffee instead of light cream (no guest has ever been heard to complain). Next morning whip whatever is left, put it in a labeled jar, and freeze it. There it stands, ready and waiting for multiple uses. It can be defrosted and turned back into coffee cream for your next guests. Or it can be defrosted, briefly whipped back, and used to garnish chocolate mousse, strawberry tarts, meringues—any dessert calling for whipped cream.

Cookie dough is a great comfort in the freezer. It defrosts quickly and makes possible fresh-baked cookies on the busiest of days.

When you bake potatoes for your family—bake an extra six or eight and stuff them all (see Index). Then freeze those that you don't use. An easy way to freeze them is to put them in the freezer on a cookie tin lined with wax paper, uncovered. When hard and frozen, they can be put in a freezer bag without getting messy.

For some reason herbs scare people. They also make food sing. If you grow them (no matter how small your garden), so much the better, but dried ones, if they have a fresh green color, are good too.

We grow chives, tarragon, oregano and lovage (perennials) as well as basil, dill, and parsley (annuals). All these grow in a small but oh so fragrant space. Throughout the summer we use them wherever possible—basil with home-grown tomatoes; chopped chives, parsley, and dill on vegetables, salads, or tiny, new, unpeeled potatoes; lovage (tastes like celery) in salad; tarragon with chicken dishes and salads; oregano is a natural for many Italian dishes. If you can't grow them, buy dried ones and use half the quantity suggested in a recipe.

The herb shelf is a good place to keep homemade bread crumbs. They are not only economical to make but will also salve your conscience as to what to do with that leftover half loaf now getting pretty hard. Cut it up and pop it in the blender. You will have bread crumbs in seconds—as fine or as coarse as you wish. If you haven't got a blender, put the bread in a paper bag and pummel it with a rolling pin. If it is not very dry, put the bread in a slow oven (200 degrees) for an hour or so. Or cut such bread into half-inch cubes and sauté in hot oil or clarified butter until a golden brown. Delicious as croutons in soup or salad. These, too, can be stored indefinitely.

No chapter on kitchen maneuvers would be complete as far as we are concerned without special emphasis on chopped fresh parsley. We use it on practically everything except desserts. To chop— we cut off the stems, wash the parsley, and put it in the blender which is then half-filled with water. Press the CHOP button and let the machine run for about thirty seconds. Pour out into a strainer, then turn parsley onto a damp, clean dishcloth or cheesecloth. Squeeze out the remaining water and spread parsley on paper towels to dry. It will emerge fluffy and bright green. Without a blender, remove the stems, *do not wash,* and chop the parsley on a wooden board with a sharp knife until it is very fine. Spoon into a damp clean dishcloth and hold under running water, squeezing and wetting a few times. One last hard squeeze, then turn out on paper towels and let dry. If you have more parsley than you want to chop —store it unwashed in a jar with screw-on top in the refrigerator where it will keep for weeks. Then chop by either method. Do not wash fresh fruits or vegetables until ready to use. Their natural coating protects, and keeps fruits and vegetables fresher if unwashed.

So much for maneuvers. Tools in hand, refrigerator stocked, we are ready to go to work.

CHAPTER 2

appetizers

There are two schools of thought about appetizers. For some, the cocktail hour (or hours) preceding a dinner party is the high spot of the evening. It goes on indefinitely while hungry guests gorge on hors d'oeuvres and there is plenty of time for refills. By the time dinner is served, nobody is very hungry, but by that time it doesn't matter.

The second school favors limiting both the quantity of appetizers and drinks, as well as the time spent consuming them. Some hostesses figure that since they have gone to the trouble of producing an elegant meal, it might be nice if the guests were in a condition to enjoy and appreciate it.

Needless to say, we favor the second school. However, under certain circumstances, there is a nice compromise. Instead of giving a dinner party, invite guests occasionally for what we call a "hearty cocktail party" lasting from about six to nine. This means that the appetizers include such filling items as steak tartare (always a hit), stuffed eggs, chicken or lobster canapés, platters of attractive cold cuts and cheese, party rye, etc. We suggest having on hand for such occasions a delicious coffee cake and/or cheesecake (both can be found in the dessert chapter) plus lots of strong, hot coffee for the last stragglers. Such a party is informal and fun for hosts and guests alike and no one, leaving such a party, need bother with dinner.

GLAZED SALTED ALMONDS

1 pound blanched almonds
1 egg white
2 tablespoons Kosher salt
1 tablespoon butter
1 teaspoon sugar
300-degree oven

Put lightly beaten egg white in a large bowl, add the nuts, and toss them until they are sticky but not wet. With a slotted spoon remove to waxed paper and sprinkle generously with salt. Place on buttered cookie sheet and bake until golden brown, turning occasionally (takes about 25–30 minutes—watch toward the end). Remove to paper towel and sprinkle lightly with sugar. Cool, then store in airtight tin until ready to serve.

PIQUANTE PECANS

½ pound shelled pecan halves
1½ tablespoons butter
1 tablespoon Worcestershire sauce
2–3 shakes of Tabasco sauce

Melt butter in saucepan, add Worcestershire sauce, and Tabasco. Remove from flame, add nuts, and shake until butter sauce is entirely absorbed. Line a cookie sheet with paper towels and pour nuts onto towels. Bake at 300 degrees for 15 minutes. Turn out on fresh paper towels and salt well.

BAKED ARTICHOKE HEARTS

1 can artichoke hearts, cut in half
¼ cup onions, chopped fine
¼ pound mushrooms, sliced
¼ cup olive oil
Juice of 1 lemon
½ cup white wine
½ teaspoon chopped chives
½ teaspoon chopped parsley
Dash of garlic powder (optional)
Salt and fresh-ground pepper

Place artichoke halves in an ovenproof dish. Combine all the other ingredients in a pan. Bring to a boil and cook over medium heat for 1 minute. Pour mixture over the artichokes and put in a 325-degree oven for 20 minutes, uncovered. Cool and refrigerate. Serve cold with toasted crackers and toothpicks.

STUFFED ARTICHOKE HEARTS

12 small artichoke hearts
6 tablespoons red caviar
3 tablespoons sour cream
1 teaspoon grated onion
Paprika
Parsley

Cut a small, straight slice from the bottom of each artichoke so that it will stand straight. Combine caviar, sour cream, and onion, and spoon into center of artichokes. Dust lightly with paprika and refrigerate until ready to serve. Garnish with parsley.

CHEESE PUFFS

1 egg yolk
½ cup grated Cheddar cheese
¼ teaspoon dry mustard
Salt
Paprika
White bread

Beat the egg yolk well, then add the cheese, mustard, salt, and paprika. Cut crusts off bread slices and cut whatever size triangle or round you prefer. Toast lightly on one side, turn, and spread the cheese mixture thickly on the untoasted side. Broil in a preheated oven until puffed and brown (about 5 minutes).

BROILED CHEESE MOUNDS

18 small, white bread rounds (about 1¼ or 1½ inches in
    diameter)
½ cup Mayonnaise
2 white onions, cut into paper-thin slices
¼–½ cup shredded Cheddar or Parmesan cheese
¼ teaspoon Worcestershire sauce
Grated Parmesan cheese

Cut bread rounds and spread lightly with mayonnaise. Cover each round with onion slices. In a bowl mix together the rest of the mayonnaise, the shredded cheese and Worcestershire sauce. Spread mixture on bread rounds, piling high in the center and sloping down to the edges. Make sure that all the bread is covered. Sprinkle with grated Parmesan and refrigerate until ready to broil. Broil quickly, very close to the flame in a preheated oven, and watch. Remove as soon as lightly browned.

PÂTÉ MAISON

1 medium onion
1 garlic clove
6 tablespoons butter
½ pound chicken livers
¼ teaspoon ground thyme
1 teaspoon chopped parsley
1 tablespoon brandy
Salt and fresh-ground pepper
1 teaspoon chopped parsley

Chop the onion, mince the garlic, and cook until onion is transparent in 2 tablespoons of butter. Add the chicken livers and sauté for 5–6 minutes, then add the thyme and parsley. Remove from heat and stir in half of the remaining butter. When butter has melted put mixture through blender, or chop well by hand and put through a sieve. When smooth, mix in the brandy and season with salt and pepper to taste. Turn out into a small china bowl. Smooth top. Melt remaining butter and pour over the top. Refrigerate for a few hours. When ready to serve, bring back to room temperature. Mix top coating of butter in pâté and serve garnished with parsley.

STEAK TARTARE #1

> 1 pound top round, tenderloin, or sirloin (fat removed, ground twice)
> Salt and fresh-ground pepper
> ½ small onion, minced
> ½ teaspoon prepared mustard
> ½ teaspoon garlic powder (optional)
> 1 teaspoon Worcestershire sauce
> 1 egg yolk
> 1 tablespoon chopped parsley
> 2 tablespoons capers

Lightly combine all the ingredients *except the parsley and capers.* Add 1–2 tablespoons ice water and mix lightly. Taste and adjust seasoning. Mound on a platter, streak lightly with a fork, sprinkle with parsley, and scatter capers over the top. Serve with unbuttered party rye.

STEAK TARTARE #2

> 1 pound top round, tenderloin, or sirloin (fat removed, ground twice)
> ½ teaspoon salt
> ¼ teaspoon fresh-ground pepper
> 1 tablespoon capers
> 1 tablespoon Worcestershire sauce
> 1 can anchovy fillets
> 1 ounce milk
> 1 pimiento
> 1 medium-sized onion, finely chopped
> Party rye or crisp white crackers

Lightly combine ground beef, salt, pepper, capers, and Worcestershire sauce. Soak anchovy fillets in milk for a few minutes. Mound meat mixture on a platter. Dry anchovies and slice them lengthwise. Starting at the center of the mound, run anchovy strips down, forming a sunburst effect. Cut pimiento into strips or circles and use for further decoration. Spoon onion around base of mound.

NOTE: This dish can be made about 2 hours ahead and kept, covered, in the refrigerator. Do not add onion until just before serving.

HERRING ELIZABETH (in Danish Mustard Sauce)

1½ pounds herring fillets
⅔ cup Mayonnaise
3 tablespoons spicy mustard
4 tablespoons dill weed
4 tablespoons chopped parsley

Cut fillets into 1-inch pieces. Set aside. Combine mayonnaise, mustard, dill weed, and parsley in a bowl.

Danish Mustard Sauce

1 tablespoon dry mustard
1 tablespoon sugar
2 tablespoons hot water
1 tablespoon Worcestershire sauce
¼ teaspoon salt
1 tablespoon vinegar
2 tablespoons salad oil

Put mustard and sugar in a bowl, add hot water, and stir until dissolved. Add Worcestershire sauce, salt, vinegar, and oil and blend well. Combine the two mixtures, stir thoroughly, then add the herring. Spoon into a jar, cover tightly, and refrigerate for twenty-four hours or more to infuse the flavors. Will keep for weeks under refrigeration.

BOLOGNA WEDGES

These are not new but somehow there is never one left at the end of a party.

1 8-ounce package of cream cheese (at room temperature)
2 tablespoons sour cream
1 teaspoon chopped chives
1 teaspoon chopped parsley
18 thin slices of small bologna

Beat the cream cheese with sour cream until it is of spreading consistency. Add chives and parsley. Taking 6 slices of bologna at a time, carefully remove the outer rind, spread cheese on bologna, and stack as in a cake. Do not put cheese on top slice. Refrigerate until 1 hour before serving. Cut into small, pie-shaped wedges (about 6 to a tower) and spear with toothpicks. Let stand at room temperature about an hour before serving.

CURRIED STUFFED EGGS

12 small or medium eggs
4 tablespoons Mayonnaise
½ teaspoon fresh lemon juice
½ teaspoon curry powder
Salt and fresh-ground pepper
Capers
Chopped parsley

Hard-cook eggs by putting them gently in boiling water to cover and cooking them slowly, uncovered, for 14 minutes. Run under cold water, peel, and cut in two the long way. Put yolks in a bowl and set whites on a platter (first cutting a thin slice from the underside of each half to prevent them from tipping). Mash yolks thoroughly with a fork or masher. Blend together mayonnaise, lemon juice, and curry powder, and add to yolks. Season to taste with salt and pepper. Fill the whites with the yolk mixture and press down lightly across the top of each with the back of a fork. Scatter 3 or 4 capers over each half and sprinkle with parsley.

STUFFED MUSHROOMS

½ pound medum-sized mushrooms
1 3-ounce package cream cheese (at room temperature)
1 tablespoon lemon juice
1 2-ounce can anchovy fillets, finely chopped
1 tablespoon chopped chives
¼ teaspoon fresh-ground pepper
2 tablespoons cream
Paprika
Parsley or watercress

Wash and peel mushrooms and remove stems (saving them for other uses). In a bowl mix together cream cheese, lemon juice, anchovies, chives, pepper, and cream and blend well. Stuff mushrooms with the mixture, filling the caps slightly higher than the edge. Dust lightly with paprika and refrigerate until ready to serve. Garnish platter with parsley or watercress.

BAKED STUFFED MUSHROOMS

¾ pound medium-sized mushrooms
1 small onion, finely chopped
1 tablespoon butter
½ cup soft bread crumbs
½ teaspoon salt
¼ teaspoon fresh-ground pepper
1 tablespoon lemon juice
1 tablespoon tomato paste
¼ teaspoon ground oregano
2–3 strips bacon
Watercress or parsley

Wash mushrooms and remove stems. Chop stems very fine. In a pan sauté onion in melted butter until transparent. Add chopped mushroom stems and sauté 2 minutes more. Place bread crumbs in a bowl with the mushrooms and onion, salt, pepper, lemon juice, tomato paste, and oregano. Mix well, and stuff the mushroom caps. Arrange on an ovenproof platter. Cut bacon into thin strips and criss-cross on top of mushrooms. The platter can now be refrig-

THE BEACH PLUM INN COOKBOOK

erated. Allow time for platter to be at room temperature for about half an hour before baking in a 400-degree oven for 20 minutes. Serve hot.

RED CAVIAR AND EGG CANAPÉS

3 tablespoons butter
12 toasted bread rounds (2½ inches in diameter)
6 tablespoons red caviar
3 hard-cooked eggs
¼ cup sour cream
3 tablespoons finely chopped onion
Fresh chopped parsley

Butter bread rounds lightly and spread with caviar. Put egg yolks through a sieve and, in a separate bowl, chop the whites quite fine. Mix together yolks, whites, sour cream, and onion, and spoon over the caviar. Sprinkle with parsley.

HOT CRABMEAT (or CHICKEN or TUNA) CANAPÉS

8 slices thin white bread
¼ cup Mayonnaise
1 teaspoon lemon juice
½ teaspoon curry powder (optional)
½ teaspoon grated onion
½ teaspoon Worcestershire sauce
8 ounces fresh crabmeat (or minced chicken or tuna)
Salt and fresh-ground pepper
2 ounces melted butter

Trim crusts from bread and roll each slice with a rolling pin until it is as flat as possible. In a bowl blend together mayonnaise, lemon juice, curry powder, onion, and Worcestershire sauce. Add the crabmeat and blend lightly. Season with salt and pepper and spread on bread. Roll up slices, brush on all sides with melted butter, and cut each roll into thirds. Bake in a 400-degree oven for 10–12 minutes, seam side down. These freeze very well. Place them rolled but uncooked on a cookie sheet in the freezer until they have frozen. Then place in freezer bags and store.

CREAM CHEESE DIP

1 8-ounce package cream cheese (at room temperature)
1 tablespoon sour cream
1 teaspoon capers
½ teaspoon dry mustard
1 tablespoon onion juice
3 small anchovies, mashed
6–8 stuffed green olives, finely chopped

Beat cream cheese with sour cream until of spreading consistency, add remaining ingredients, blend lightly, and sprinkle with paprika. Serve with toasted crackers.

TOAST CRISPS

¾ stick of butter
2 cloves of garlic
1 loaf thin-sliced white bread
Parmesan cheese

Put butter and peeled, slightly crushed, garlic cloves in a saucepan and heat until butter bubbles. Remove from stove and let stand three hours. Discard the garlic. Remove crusts from bread and, with a cookie cutter, cut rounds about 1 inch in diameter. Arrange on a cookie sheet, brush with garlic butter and sprinkle generously with Parmesan cheese. Lightly salt each round and bake in a 350-degree oven until crisp (about 10 minutes). These keep for weeks in a tightly covered jar.

HOT TARTLETS

1 cake cream cheese (3 ounces) at room temperature
¼ pound butter
1 cup flour (sift before measuring)

Blend all the ingredients together, form into a ball, wrap in wax paper, and refrigerate for at least an hour—this dough will keep for weeks under refrigeration.

THE BEACH PLUM INN COOKBOOK

Filling

2 tablespoons butter
4 mushrooms, finely chopped
1 small onion, finely chopped
Salt and fresh-ground pepper
1 tablespoon chopped parsey

Egg Wash

1 egg, beaten with 1 teaspoon water

To Make Filling: Melt butter in pan and sauté onion until transparent. Add mushrooms and sauté over low heat for 2–3 minutes more. Season to taste.

To Make Tartlets: Roll out dough to ⅛ inch thickness. Cut into circles 4 inches in diameter. Brush edges with egg wash and place about a teaspoonful of filling in the center. Fold in two and press edges together with the back of a fork. Brush lightly with egg wash. Bake in a preheated 400-degree oven for 12 minutes, or until lightly golden. Serve hot or cold. These can be made a day ahead up to the point of baking and are always a hit. The variations for filling are endless. Combine chopped chicken or lobster with a little curried mayonnaise or fill with chicken livers or sausage meat or whatever you have at hand that tastes good.

Turn these tartlets into a dessert by filling with mincemeat, orange marmalade, strawberry preserves, etc. When making them into a dessert add a light sprinkling of sugar on top immediately after brushing with egg wash.

soup, soup, beautiful soup

These days, when entertaining, we balk at first courses. In this day
of do-it-yourself, it is "the straw that breaks . . ." By the time a
hostess-cook has produced delicious appetizers and lined up a
splendid dinner to follow, maneuvering a first course can be a dis-
aster and surely a nuisance. But if we are going to make an exception, it will be for soup. Winter or summer, it is the easiest and
pleasantest first course.

It is also a fine luncheon dish. Gone are the days of elaborate
luncheon parties. Today most of us have neither the time nor the
inclination to bother with them. But a cup of homemade soup, a
tasty sandwich, and a delicious cookie or two can be a banquet.
Soup can also be a star performer at a Sunday night supper party.

While we're on the subject of soup—this is as good a time as any to mention garnish. Food, enhanced by almost any garnish, is to a meal what a bowl of fresh flowers is to a room. Not absolutely necessary, but what a difference both make.

Any dish is improved by being attractively presented. An ordinary platter of cold cuts gains positive allure when decorated with a bunch of parsley or watercress, a few pickles, or even fresh lettuce leaves. How much greater the possibilities when it comes to glamorizing soup.

Take your choice or rather use whatever you happen to have at hand. Got some stale bread? Trim off the crusts, cut the slices into ½-inch cubes, and sauté in oil until they are brown on both sides. If you like, the pan can be rubbed with garlic before adding the oil. Drain the cubes on a paper towel and, when dry, store in an airtight tin until ready to use.

Chopped parsley, chives, or dill have an affinity for almost any soup. Or add a slice of hard-cooked egg, a thin slice of lemon, some chopped cucumber or diced avocado, a dollop of sour cream, chopped watercress, a dash of paprika—any one of them will add interest and color to your soup. Some soups are improved by the addition of a little sherry or Madeira, and all soups are improved by the removal of fat. If your soup is made ahead—store it in the refrigerator where the fat will rise to the top and harden, thus making it easy to remove. If soup is made at the last minute, drop in a few cubes of ice (to which the fat will cling and can easily be removed). Or skim off the fat with several pieces of paper towel, running each across the top of the soup, then throw it away, and repeat.

While many fine soups use water or milk as the basic liquid stock, most of our soups begin with beef or chicken stock. With additional seasoning, these may be used as soups by themselves, or as the base of many gravies and sauces.

If you are a perfectionist, *if* you are willing to do a little extra work, you will find three basic recipes for Beef Stock, Light; Beef Stock, Dark; and Chicken Stock at the end of this chapter. However, we must admit that your soups, sauces, and gravies will be excellent if you use any fine brand of consommé, bouillon, or soup base available in a good market.

All but cream soups freeze extremely well and are a boon to have on hand. Here are some of our favorites.

CHICKEN BRUNOISE

    1 onion
    1 carrot
    1 large stalk of celery
    1½ quarts chicken stock
    2 egg yolks
    1 tablespoon fresh lemon juice
    Salt and fresh-ground pepper
    Chopped parsley or dill

Cut the vegetables into small dice (about ¼ inch) and simmer in chicken stock for 30 minutes. In a bowl beat the egg yolks and lemon juice. Pour a little of the hot soup over the yolks, beating constantly with a whisk, then pour this mixture into the rest of the soup. Heat over a low flame—*do not let boil.* Add salt and pepper to taste. Pour into warmed cups and garnish with a sprinkling of fresh chopped parsley or dill.

CUCUMBER SOUP

    4 cucumbers
    1 large onion
    1½ quarts chicken stock
    2 ounces butter
    3 tablespoons flour
    Salt and fresh-ground pepper
    ½ cup white wine

Garnish

    ½ cucumber, finely diced
    ½ cup sour cream
    Chopped chives

Peel and split cucumbers into four slices the long way (reserving half of one for garnish). Chop coarsely. Chop onion very fine and simmer cucumbers and onion in chicken stock for 30 minutes.

Cool. Purée in blender at low speed (not filling container more than half full at any time) or rub through strainer or food mill. In a pan melt butter, stir in flour, and cook over medium heat for 2 minutes. Remove from flame and ladle in a little hot stock, stirring constantly. Add to soup pot and stir with a wire whisk until it comes to a boil. Let simmer about 5 minutes, during which bring wine to a boil. Add wine, check for seasoning. For garnish—add remaining uncooked half cucumber (diced) to sour cream. Pour soup into hot cups, add cucumber-sour cream mixture, and sprinkle with chopped chives.

This soup is also delicious when served very cold.

LEMON SOUP

2 ounces butter (½ stick)
1 medium onion, finely chopped
2½ tablespoons flour
1½ quarts chicken stock
2 lemons
Salt and fresh-ground pepper
3 egg yolks
1 cup medium cream
Fresh chopped parsley

Melt butter, add onion, and cook until transparent. Remove from flame and stir in flour until well blended. Add warm chicken stock. Stir well with whisk. Heat stock to boiling, stirring as it thickens. Reduce heat to simmer. With vegetable parer remove yellow zest* from one lemon. Add zest and juice of one lemon to soup. Simmer 20 minutes. Strain and taste. The lemon flavor should be very delicate. Season with salt and pepper to taste. In a small bowl beat egg yolks, then beat in cream. Ladle some hot soup into egg mixture, stirring to prevent curdling. Add egg mixture to soup, stirring constantly. At this point keep soup hot, but do not allow to boil. For garnish, cut very thin slices of lemon from second lemon. Dip lemon slices into chopped parsley and gently drop parsleyed lemon into hot soup. Serve at once.

* Zest is the very thin yellow part of lemon peel and does not include any white.

CREAM OF CELERY AND APPLE SOUP

Don't be afraid to try this—it's very good!

1 large or 2 medium bunches of celery
1 medium-sized onion
3 ounces butter
3 cups milk
2 cups water (or chicken stock)
2 bay leaves
6 peppercorns
1 cup milk
3 tablespoons flour
Salt
2 egg yolks
½ cup heavy cream
1 large apple (diced with skin on and sprinkled with lemon juice to
    preserve color)

Chop celery and onion quite fine. Melt 1 ounce of the butter in a pan, add the vegetables, cover tightly, and cook very slowly for 25–30 minutes (or until vegetables are soft). Meanwhile put milk in another pan with bay leaves and peppercorns, bring slowly to a boil and simmer 3–4 minutes. Strain into a bowl. Wash pan, add remaining 2 ounces butter, and, when melted, off flame, stir in flour. Cook for 3 minutes, then add the milk and water (or stock). Return to fire and stir to smooth texture as it comes to a boil. Reduce heat and simmer 5 minutes. Add 1 cup milk to the celery-onion mixture and purée in blender at lowest speed. Add to soup, bring to a boil, simmer gently, and correct seasoning. Beat egg yolks, add cream, blend well, then add a few tablespoons of soup, stirring well. Pour this mixture into the rest of the soup. *Do not boil again.* Reheat, if not using at once, in a double boiler. Serve with diced apple sprinkled over the top.

HERBED MUSHROOM SOUP

3 tablespoons butter
2 medium-sized onions, finely chopped
½ pound mushrooms, very finely chopped
2 tablespoons flour

1 quart plus 1 cup chicken stock
2 tablespoons rice, uncooked
1 bay leaf
Sat and fresh-ground pepper
2 tablespoons chopped parsley
2 tablespoons chopped fresh mint or ½ teaspoon dried mint

Melt butter and sauté onions over medium heat until golden. Add mushrooms and sauté for 5 minutes more. Remove from flame, add flour, and mix well. Return to flame and cook slowly for 3 minutes. Heat stock until just simmering, remove from flame and add onion-mushroom mixture, stirring constantly with a whisk. Return to flame and bring to a boil. Add rice and bay leaf and simmer 17 minutes. Remove bay leaf and season to taste with salt and pepper. Add parsley and mint. Serve hot.

CREAM OF WATERCRESS

1½ ounces butter
2 medium-sized onions, finely chopped
2 bunches watercress, chopped
2½ tablespoons flour
1½ quarts milk
Salt and fresh-ground pepper

Liaison

2 egg yolks
½ cup heavy cream

In a pan melt butter, add onions and watercress, cover tightly, and cook over low heat for 10 minutes. Remove from heat, add flour. Cook for 2–3 minutes over medium heat. Bring milk to just under boil and pour over mixture, stirring gently. Simmer about 20 minutes. Cool a little, then purée in blender or rub through a sieve. Taste and correct seasoning.

Beat together egg yolks and cream. Add a little hot soup to this mixture, stirring rapidly to prevent curdling. When well blended, add egg and cream mixture to the soup, stirring well. Keep hot, but do not let boil. If not serving at once, refrigerate. When ready to serve heat gently, or use double boiler. Serve with croutons.

TOMATO ORANGE SOUP
Unusual and very good

2 pounds fresh skinned tomatoes (or a 30-ounce can of tomatoes)
1 quart chicken stock
1 medium onion, thinly sliced
1 carrot, scraped and thinly sliced
1 strip lemon rind
1 bay leaf
1 teaspoon salt
½ teaspoon fresh-ground pepper
½ teaspoon sugar
1½ ounces butter
3 tablespoons flour
Juice of 1 orange
2 tablespoons chopped parsley

Cut up tomatoes and put in soup pot with chicken stock, onion, carrot, lemon rind, bay leaf, salt, pepper, and sugar. Bring to a boil, then simmer for 30–35 minutes. In a large pan melt butter; remove from flame and add flour. Blend well, then add ½ cup of the hot soup, stirring constantly. Bring to a boil, cook a minute or two, then add the rest of the soup and boil gently 2 minutes. Cool a little, remove lemon rind, and purée soup in blender (careful not to do too much at a time). Return soup to pan, add orange juice, and correct seasoning. Ladle soup into hot soup plates and sprinkle with parsley. Also very good with croutons.

CREAM OF SPINACH SOUP

2 packages frozen spinach or 1¼ pounds fresh
1 onion, finely chopped
3 cups water
3 cups milk
2 ounces butter
2 tablespoons flour
⅛ teaspoon nutmeg
Salt and fresh-ground pepper
½ cup heavy cream

Garnish

2 hard-cooked eggs, chopped

If using fresh spinach wash in cold water. Place spinach and chopped onion in the 3 cups of water; bring to a boil. Reduce heat and simmer for 15 minutes. Add milk and cook for 5 minutes more. Cool a little, then purée in blender. Return to soup pot. In a pan melt butter, stir in flour, and cook over medium heat for 3 minutes, stirring to thicken. Ladle in one cup of soup, stir until smooth, then add mixture to the rest of the soup. Bring to a boil and stir until smooth. Reduce heat and simmer gently. Add nutmeg, salt, pepper, and cream. Pour into hot cups and garnish with a sprinkling of chopped egg.

POTAGE JARDINIÈRE (purée)

2 ounces butter
2 medium onions, finely chopped
2 potatoes, peeled and thinly sliced
3 celery sticks, cut up
1 large carrot, thinly sliced
1 cup fresh green beans
1 quart plus 1 cup chicken stock
1 cup fresh peas
¼ head lettuce, shredded
1 teaspoon celery salt
½ teaspoon salt
¼ teaspoon fresh-ground pepper
2–3 ounces sherry
Croutons
Parsley

Melt butter, sauté onions until transparent. Prepare vegetables. Place potatoes, celery, carrot, and green beans in cold stock and bring to a boil slowly. Simmer 15 minutes and add peas and lettuce. Simmer 30 minutes more. Cool soup a bit and put through blender to purée. Purée thoroughly for a smooth texture. Add both salts, pepper, and sherry. Simmer. Serve with croutons and parsley garnish.

NOTE: Spinach may be used in place of lettuce.

MENEMSHA FISH CHOWDER

Aficionados of fish chowder request this recipe over and over again. Served with herbed toast and a salad, it makes a fine supper. A blueberry or peach pie does no harm as a finale. This recipe was requested by Gourmet *magazine.*

Stock

    1 quart water
    1 onion, sliced
    1 stick celery, coarsely chopped
    ¾ pound fresh fish bones—whatever you can obtain, such as
        fluke, cod, bass, sole, haddock, flounder, etc. Be sure it's not
        an oily fish.
    1 bay leaf
    6 peppercorns
    Parsley stems
    ½ teaspoon salt
    2 cups white wine

Put water in a large pot and add all the ingredients *except the wine.* Bring to a boil and simmer for 10 minutes, then skim. Add 2 tablespoons cold water, bring to a boil, and again skim. Simmer for about 30 minutes. Add wine, simmer 2–3 minutes more, remove from heat, and strain into a bowl. Let cool and then refrigerate until ready to use.

Chowder

    2 ounces butter
    1 medium onion, finely chopped
    1 stick celery, finely chopped
    2 tablespoons flour
    1 quart hot fish stock (from above)
    2 raw potatoes, peeled and diced
    ½ pound cod, haddock, or flounder fillets, cut into small pieces
    ½–¾ pound bass (or other firm fish) cut into small pieces
    ½ teaspoon celery salt
    Salt and fresh-ground pepper
    2 cups milk
    ½ cup light cream
    Paprika
    Oyster crackers

Melt butter in large skillet, and sauté onion and celery until golden. Off the heat, stir in flour, blend well, bring to a boil for a minute or two, then hold. In another pan bring fish stock to a boil, add diced potatoes, and cook over medium heat until potatoes are barely done. Add onion-celery-flour mixture and bring to a boil, then simmer for 2–3 minutes. Add cut-up fish and simmer another 10 minutes. Season to taste with celery salt, salt, and pepper. Add warm milk and cream and heat thoroughly *but do not boil.* Pour into warmed soup cups, sprinkle with parsley, and serve with a side bowl of oyster crackers.

GAZPACHO

3 large cucumbers, peeled and cut into tiny dice
3 teaspoons salt
1 30-ounce can tomatoes (or 2 pounds fresh, peeled and diced)
2 tablespoons chopped pimiento
1 large onion, or 3 whole scallions, chopped
3 tablespoons cider vinegar
4 tablespoons olive oil
1 clove garlic, minced
1 teaspoon sugar
½ teaspoon cumin
½ quart chicken stock
1 cup water
Salt and pepper to taste
2 tablespoons chopped chives

Place small-diced cucumbers in bowl, sprinkle on salt and let stand 10 minutes. Add all the ingredients but the salt, pepper, and chives. Mix gently but thoroughly; check the taste and season with salt and pepper as needed. Chill soup by placing the bowl, covered, in refrigerator for several hours. Serve in chilled soup cups, garnished with a sprinkling of chopped chives.

NOTE: As vinegar comes in varying strengths and cucumbers may require more salt, add more seasoning if needed.

SHRIMP AND POTATO SOUP

Shrimp Stock

    8 ounces shrimp, cleaned†
    1 onion, chopped fine
    1 bay leaf
    2 or 3 whole cloves
    ½ lemon, thinly sliced
    1 stick celery, chopped fine

Cook shrimp in one quart salted water until just boiled. Cool at once in cold running water. Set aside cooking water. Combine all ingredients except shrimp and add to the hot liquid in which shrimp was boiled. Bring back to boil, then simmer 45 minutes. Strain and use. Stock will keep well under refrigeration for a few days.

Soup

    1 pound potatoes
    3 ounces leeks, or 1 medium to large onion
    1 quart shrimp‡ stock
    ½ stick butter (2 ounces)
    ½ teaspoon paprika
    1 egg yolk
    ½ cup warm milk
    Salt and fresh-ground pepper
    Croutons
    Chopped parsley

Peel and slice potatoes. Slice leeks or onion. Place potatoes and onion in pot with stock. Bring to boil, then simmer for 20 minutes. Cool, then purée through blender. Melt half of the butter. Chop shrimp into small pieces and sauté lightly in butter. Sprinkle with paprika. Return stock to clean pot. Add shrimp. Bring slowly to boil, then reduce heat to simmer. Beat in dots of the remaining half of the butter. Beat egg yolk, add milk, and beat together. Add some hot stock to the egg mix and beat. Then add all to hot stock pot and stir. *Do not reboil.* Check for seasoning. Serve with croutons and chopped parsley garnish.

† In some markets one can find peeled, deveined, frozen shrimp in broken pieces which are of excellent quality and considerably lower in cost.
‡ Fish or chicken stock may also be used.

CLAM CHOWDER BEACH PLUM INN

This is a hearty soup which, accompanied by a salad and dessert, makes a fine Sunday night supper. It can be prepared a day in advance, refrigerated, and slowly reheated.

12–14 hard-shell clams (quahogs), about 4–5 pounds in shells
1 cup water
3 slices bacon
1 tablespoon butter
2 medium onions, chopped
2 sticks celery, diced
3 tablespoons flour

Wash quahogs carefully, using several rinses of fresh water. Place in tightly covered pot with the water. Heat until quahogs open, then remove from heat and allow to cool. Fry bacon in skillet until crisp. Remove from pan to paper towel and set aside. Add the butter, onions, and celery to bacon fat and sauté until lightly golden. Stir in the flour and cook over medium heat for about 3 minutes. Set aside.

2 large Idaho, or 4 medium, potatoes, peeled and diced
1 pint plus 1 cup cold water
2 tomatoes, skinned and chopped (optional)
1 teaspoon celery salt
½ teaspoon ground thyme
Pepper to taste
4 ounces good dry white wine (optional)
1 cup hot milk
1 cup hot medium cream
Salt to taste
Chopped parsley for garnish
Oyster crackers

Remove quahogs from shells. Reserve broth and strain into a pot. Discard shells. Add potatoes and the water to broth and boil for 6–8 minutes. Reduce heat, stir in the flour mixture. Stir as you bring to boil, then reduce heat to simmer. Add chopped tomatoes, celery salt, thyme, pepper, and wine. While simmering add finely chopped quahog meats and finely chopped bacon. Stir in the hot milk and cream. Check for flavor. Here you may or may not add salt depending on the saltiness of the quahogs. Serve garnished with chopped parsley and a side dish of oyster crackers.

Beach Plum Inn is a seaside resort, and fresh quahogs and clams are always available. There are, however, canned clams available which will make a good chowder.

BEEF STOCK—LIGHT

2 pounds beef and veal bones
1½ quarts cold water
1 onion, peeled and cut up
1 carrot, sliced
1 stick celery with leaves, sliced
1 bay leaf
A few crushed peppercorns
A few sprigs thyme
A few crushed stems of parsley
2 cloves
½ teaspoon salt

Wash bones in cold water, then place in the cold water and slowly bring to a boil. Reduce heat to simmer and skim the scum off the top. Turn up heat to slow boil, add a few tablespoons of cold water which will bring more scum up to top. Reduce to simmer and skim again. Repeat if needed. Now add the vegetables and aromatic herbs and salt. Simmer for 3–4 hours, occasionally adding water to bring to original level. Cool a bit. Put through cheesecloth strainer or fine mesh sieve.

This stock can serve as a base for many soups. It will keep for three or four days under refrigeration, or indefinitely if frozen. Makes about one quart.

BEEF STOCK—DARK

2½ pounds beef bones
1 medium to large onion, sliced
1 large carrot, sliced
1 large stick celery with leaves, sliced

1½ quarts cold water
1 8-ounce can tomatoes
1 bay leaf
A few crushed peppercorns
A few sprigs thyme
Crushed parsley with stems
2 or 3 whole cloves
½ teaspoon salt

Wash bones. Place on roasting pan or sheet pan in a 375-degree oven and roast for about one hour, turning bones from time to time so they will evenly brown. Pour a bit of fat from bones into skillet and sauté onion, carrot, and celery until golden to deep brown. Now take up bones and place in soup pot, add water, tomatoes, sautéed vegetables, and aromatic herbs and salt. Bring to a boil, skim top, and simmer uncovered 4 hours. Stock will reduce by about half, resulting in about one quart of stock. Strain through cheesecloth or fine mesh sieve.

Stock is now ready for many uses. Refrigerate.

By boiling stock every 4–5 days, it will keep indefinitely in refrigerator. It will also freeze well.

CHICKEN STOCK (BROTH)

1 4–5-pound chicken (whole or cut up)
2–3 sets uncooked giblets, cut up
2½ quarts cold water
1 carrot, chopped
1 onion, sliced
1 stick celery, cut up
1 bay leaf
A few sprigs parsley
½ teaspoon thyme
½ teaspoon salt
¼ teaspoon fresh-ground pepper

Brown the chicken and the giblets in 425-degree oven for about 15–20 minutes. Place chicken in the water in large pot and slowly bring to boil. Reduce heat to simmer and skim off the top. Add a

few tablespoons of cold water and repeat, until all scum is removed. Add the vegetables and herbs. Bring to boil, skim top
again, then simmer for 1½–2 hours, or until chicken is done.
Remove chicken and giblets, strain through cheesecloth or fine
mesh sieve. When cooled, remove fat from top of stock. Pour stock
into container and refrigerate.

The boiled chicken may be served in numerous ways, ranging
from hot chicken in broth to cold chicken salad, etc.

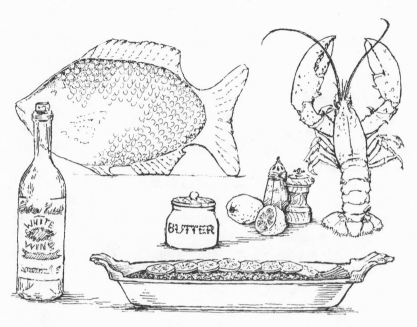

fish

Within the last few years fish has come into its own. No longer is it the inexpensive stepchild with which we balance the family budget or protein requirements. Instead, it provides an unlimited range of delicious meals.

Fish can be transformed into broths, chowders, or bouilla-baisses. It can be poached, steamed, fried, baked, broiled, and smoked. It can serve as an appetizer, a first course, or the main dish for a meal.

We on Martha's Vineyard are fortunate in having available a great variety of treasures from the sea. From tiny bay scallops to fillet of flounder, from swordfish steaks to oysters, from striped bass to halibut, with lobsters, crabs, sole, and much else besides—we enjoy them all at different times of the year. If you, too, like fish, keep on hand a bowl of clarified butter (which has dozens of uses other than for cooking fish). It has a special affinity for fish and does not burn. Or you can use a mixture of butter and oil.

CLARIFIED BUTTER

Clarify whatever amount you wish; it will keep for weeks, tightly covered, in the refrigerator.

In a saucepan, melt butter over low heat and let cook a minute or two after it is melted. Remove from heat and let stand a few minutes. Then skim off the frothy substance that has formed at the top until you have clear, yellow liquid. Cool, then store in refrigerator to harden.

When ready to use, cut or punch a hole in the butter and pour off the small amount of liquid that has accumulated underneath. Use whatever amount you need and store balance, covered, in refrigerator. It will also freeze well. Since it does not burn, it is especially good when cooking chicken, shrimp, veal, etc., or serving lobster with butter sauce. One pound of butter will yield approximately ¾ pound clarified butter.

MENEMSHA BAKED SCROD

> 2½–3 pounds fillet of cod or haddock
> ½ stick butter
> Juice of ½ lemon
> 4 tablespoons white bread crumbs
> Salt and fresh-ground pepper
> 6 lemon wedges
> Chopped parsley

Cut scrod fillets into portions. Dry fish and set lightly on buttered baking pan. Melt butter and lemon juice together and brush or spoon over fish. Sprinkle on the bread crumbs. Season with salt and fresh-ground pepper. Place under broiler about 5 minutes to color fish until golden brown. Remove from broiler and brush on a little more butter. Set oven at 375 degrees and bake for 15–18 minutes. Remove to warmed platter and serve with lemon wedges. Garnish with parsley.

FISH AMANDINE

Amandine

    4 tablespoons butter
    6 tablespoons blanched slivered or sliced almonds

Melt butter, add almonds, and cook over medium heat until a golden color. Set aside.

    3 pounds fillet of fluke, flounder, or sole
    4 tablespoons Clarified Butter
    Juice of ½ lemon
    ½ teaspoon salt
    ½ teaspoon fresh-ground pepper
    2 tablespoons chopped parsley
    6 lemon wedges

Heat half of the clarified butter in a pan suitable for broiling. Add fish, and sauté gently for about 2–3 minutes over medium heat. Remove from heat and drizzle over lemon juice. Add the remaining butter. Season with salt and pepper and broil about 4 inches from flame for 6 minutes, or until golden. With wide spatula gently remove fish to warm platter. Spoon on the almonds, run under broiler for a minute more, garnish with parsley, and serve with lemon wedges.

HERBED BROILED SWORDFISH

    3 pounds fresh swordfish, cut about 1¼ inches thick
    1 cup French Dressing

Place fish in pan suitable for broiling and pour on French dressing. Cover with wax paper (or plastic film) and place in refrigerator. Marinate for about 2 hours, turning once.

Herbed Butter Sauce

    1 cup Clarified Butter
    Juice of 1 lemon
    1 tablespoon chopped parsley
    1 tablespoon chopped chives
    1 tablespoon chopped tarragon
    Salt and fresh-ground pepper
    6 lemon wedges

Melt the clarified butter, add lemon juice, parsley, chives, and tarragon. Season with salt and pepper. Set aside. About ½ hour before broiling remove fish from refrigerator. Broil in the marinade about 4 inches from heat. When fish is golden brown, remove from broiler and turn over carefully. Broil second side, which will take about half the time. Remove from broiler. With a sharp paring knife cut away the skin. It will come away easily. Cut fish into uniform portions, allowing two slices per person. Set on warmed platter and spoon on the heated herbed butter. Serve with wedges of lemon.

NOTE: Use any leftover fish for salad (as you would for tuna).

POACHED FILLET OF SOLE BONNE FEMME

1 tablespoon butter
2 pounds fillet of thin sole
¼ cup dry white wine
Juice of ½ lemon
Few slices onion
6–8 peppercorns
1 bay leaf

Butter 1½–2-inch-deep ovenproof pan. Roll up fish fillets and put in pan. Add wine, lemon juice, onion slices, peppercorns, and bay leaf. Cover tightly with buttered paper and aluminum wrap over the paper. Place in 325-degree oven and poach for about 18 minutes. While fish is poaching, prepare sauce:

Bonne Femme Sauce

4 tablespoons butter
1½ cups sliced mushrooms
3 tablespoons flour
1 cup hot milk
½ teaspoon celery salt
½ teaspoon salt
¼ teaspoon fresh-ground pepper
4 tablespoons heavy cream (optional)

Garnish

2 tablespoons chopped parsley
6 lemon wedges

Melt butter in pan and sauté mushrooms about 4 minutes. Stir in the flour over medium heat and cook for about 2 minutes. Add the hot milk, bring to a boil to thicken, stirring constantly. Add celery salt, salt, pepper, and heavy cream. Set aside but keep warm.

Remove fish from oven. Remove cover and carefully strain about 1 cup of fish juice into bonne femme sauce. Keep fish warm in oven. Slowly bring sauce to boil; check for seasoning. Remove portion of fish from pan and place on warm platter. Spoon hot sauce over fish. Sprinkle with chopped parsley and serve with lemon wedges.

NOTE: A variation of this dish can be created by stuffing the fillets. Prepare 1 cup cooked shrimp, crabmeat, or lobster meat, chopped fine. These may be used alone or in any combination. Place 1 full teaspoon on each fish fillet before rolling. Roll fillets around seafood filling and proceed with recipe as above.

STRIPED BASS WITH LOBSTER SAUCE

Our number 1 fish dish!

Make lobster sauce first:

5 tablespoons butter
4 tablespoons flour
1½ cups stock made from lobster shells
¼ cup dry white wine, heated
5–6 ounces cooked lobster meat, diced
1 teaspoon celery salt
¼ teaspoon paprika
2 tablespoons chopped chives
¼ cup heavy cream, warmed
Salt and fresh-ground pepper to taste

Melt butter, stir in flour, and cook over medium heat for 3 minutes. Add stock, bring to a boil, stirring with wire whisk until smooth and thick. Add wine, then lobster meat, celery salt, paprika, and chives. Bring to boil, reduce heat, then add heavy cream. Season with salt and pepper. Place in double boiler and keep hot without boiling.

Striped Bass
    3–3½ pounds striped bass fillets, cut into 6 portions
    ⅓ cup Clarified Butter
    Juice of 1 lemon
    6 tablespoons white bread crumbs
    ½ teaspoon paprika
    6 lemon wedges
    2 tablespoons chopped parsley

Cooking time is estimated for a fillet about 1¼–1½ inches thick. Melt half the butter in large skillet. Place fillets, skin side down, in pan on top of stove and sauté over medium heat for about 5 minutes. Remove skillet from top of stove and put under broiler about 4 inches from heat. Broil for about 6 minutes. Remove pan from broiler, brush remaining butter over the fish, add the lemon juice, and sprinkle on the bread crumbs. Return to broiler. Fish will now color quickly. Remove when golden brown. Add a dash of paprika. Remove fish to warmed platter. Spoon lobster sauce over fish. Serve with lemon wedges and pinch of parsley.

    NOTE: Lobster sauce prepared in advance will keep in refrigerator for hours. Reheat slowly in double boiler, stirring a few times.

BAKED FISH (Stuffed or served whole)

Many species of fish lend themselves to being cooked and served whole. The finished product when brought to the table can present a most attractive appearance and is delicious. Since there is little waste in serving a whole fish, it has the added charm of being economical.

    The fish in our waters suited to baking whole are striped bass, weakfish (also known as sea trout), bluefish, and small cod. A few species from other areas which will bake equally well are red snapper, king mackerel, lake bass, carp, salmon, and salmon trout. To serve 6 we suggest buying a 4–5-pound fish.

BAKED STUFFED FISH

4½–5-pound fish (split, boned, and head and tail removed)
1 teaspoon salt
¾ teaspoon pepper
2 cloves of garlic, minced
3 tablespoons oil
2 cups white bread crumbs
4 slices of bacon
½ cup green onions, finely chopped
½ cup celery, finely chopped
4 tablespoons butter, melted
¾ cup dry white wine
¾ teaspoon parsley

Garnish

½ teaspoon paprika
Fresh parsley sprigs
Lemon wedges

Preheat oven to 400 degrees. Wash and wipe fish dry. Rub inside and out with pepper, salt, garlic, and oil. Place crumbs in a bowl. Sauté bacon until crisp, then crumble it into the bread crumbs, reserving 2 tablespoons of bacon fat in which to sauté the onions and celery over medium heat until just turning golden (about 10 minutes). Add vegetables to bread crumbs and bacon, then parsley, half of the melted butter and 3 tablespoons wine. Mix lightly and stuff mixture into cavity of the fish. Sew or seal with skewers and pat fish back into original shape.

Brush baking pan with the balance of the butter. Place fish on the pan and bake for about 40 minutes. Pour the balance of the wine over the fish, reduce heat to 325 degrees, and bake about 30 minutes longer (or until fish flakes easily when tested with a fork). During the last 30 minutes baste fish with pan juices once or twice.

Remove fish from oven and allow to cool a little before transferring it to warmed serving platter. Garnish lightly with paprika and surround with parsley sprigs and lemon wedges. Serve at the table.

BAKED WHOLE FISH

1 fish (approximately 5 pounds)
Salt and fresh-ground pepper
1 stick of butter, melted
1 teaspoon ground basil
1 large onion, thinly sliced
2 tomatoes, thinly sliced
Juice of ½ lemon
½ teaspoon ground oregano
1 lemon, thinly sliced
2 tablespoons fresh chopped parsley

Preheat oven to 400 degrees. Have fish cleaned and scales removed, but left whole. Some like the head and tail off—some on—it is your choice. Sprinkle salt and pepper into the cavity, place fish on greased baking pan, and brush with melted butter. Sprinkle salt, pepper, and basil over the fish. Bake for about 25 minutes, brushing butter on twice. Remove from oven and turn oven up to 425 degrees. Arrange onion slices, neatly overlapping, on top of fish, then the tomato slices over the onion and squeeze fresh lemon juice over tomatoes. Dribble butter over the tomato slices, sprinkle on the oregano, return to oven, and bake about 20 minutes longer (or until fish flakes easily when tested with a fork). Remove from oven and carefully place fish on a large, warmed platter. Cover lightly with a towel, allowing fish to cool a few degrees before bringing it to the table. This will make the carving easier. Remove towel, surround fish with lemon slices, garnish with parsley and serve whole at the table.

NOTE: Weakfish, codfish, sea bass, red snapper, salmon, salmon trout and lake bass are all lean fish and may be prepared in the same manner.

Bluefish, king mackerel, and carp are fatty fish and require less butter in preparation as the fish supplies most of the required moisture.

BROILED MACKEREL

We've heard a lot of people say, "I don't care for mackerel" and then come back for seconds.

6 mackerel fillets, about 8 ounces each
2 tablespoons oil
Salt and fresh-ground pepper
6 lemon wedges
Parsley sprig

Lightly oil broiling pan. Place fillets, skin side up on pan and, with fingers, rub balance of oil over the skin. Place under preheated broiler 4–6 inches from heat. Broil for about 5 minutes, until partly cooked and skin begins to blister. Turn fillets over, sprinkle with salt and pepper, and continue broiling until crisp and golden brown. No basting required. Remove to warm plates and serve with lemon wedges. Garnish with parsley sprig.

BREAKFAST FISH

If you've never had fish for breakfast, you've missed something. Especially on Sunday morning, accompanied by crisp bacon.

Fried Fillet of Flounder, Sole, or Porgy—serve about 4 oz. per portion for breakfast. Or more if you wish.

1½ pounds fresh fillets of flounder, sole, or porgy
½ cup oil (or fat) for frying
1 cup bread crumbs, seasoned with salt and pepper
6 lemon wedges
Parsley sprig
12 strips crisp bacon

Cut fillets into medium-sized pieces (about 1–1½ inches wide). Heat oil in heavy frying pan, dredge fillets in seasoned bread crumbs, and fry, uncrowded in pan, until crisp and golden brown on both sides. Remove to absorbent paper and keep warm. Serve with lemon wedges, parsley, and bacon.

BOILED LOBSTER

In our opinion, this simple method of preparing lobster is the best. When boiling 6 lobsters use a very large pot holding at least 3 or 4 gallons of water. Add 2 tablespoons of salt per gallon. Heat water to a rolling boil.

> 6 live lobsters, about 1½ pounds each
> 6 lemon wedges
> 6 sprigs of parsley
> 1¼ cups Clarified Butter

Place live lobsters head first into the boiling water and return water to a rolling boil. Reduce heat, cover pot, and then cook for about 16 minutes. Remove lobsters with tongs, and place on a table covered with newspapers. Cover with towel and allow to cool for about 5 minutes.

Set lobster shell side up on cutting board. Hold tail firmly, and with a heavy knife cut tail vertically. Open tail gently and remove the vein. Remove pegs or bands around claws. Place on warm platter. Fold claws over each other and place a lemon wedge between claws. Put a sprig of parsley in split tail. Serve at once with 1½ ounces clarified butter per person.

BAKED STUFFED LOBSTER

6 lobsters, about 1¼–1½ pounds each. Ask the man at the fish market to split underside of lobsters without breaking the shell and remove sac and vein. Break off large claws, and remove liver and coral from cavity of lobster and store in refrigerator, until needed.

Stuffing

> 3 quarts water
> 1 tablespoon salt
> ½ pound shrimp, peeled and deveined
> 2–2½ cups bread crumbs
> 1 stick butter, melted
> Liver and coral
> ½ teaspoon salt
> ½ teaspoon fresh-ground pepper

2 tablespoons chopped parsley
Juice of 1 lemon
½ cup oil

Boil 3 quarts water with 1 tablespoon salt. Place lobster claws in the boiling water and when water returns to a boil, add the shrimp and bring to boil again. Allow to boil for about 1 minute. Refresh lobster claws and shrimp in cold water. Break claws and remove meat. Cut lobster claw meat and shrimp into about ½-inch dice, and place in a bowl. Add the bread crumbs, reserving about ¼ cup. Pour on melted butter, add the liver and coral, and add salt, pepper, and chopped parsley. Gently mix. Place lobsters shell side down on cookie pans. Fill cavity and tail of lobsters with stuffing. Brush oil over lobster shells. Squeeze on the juice of one lemon. Place lobsters on pans so the head of one lobster will rest on the tip of a tail of another. This will prevent lobster tails from curling up during baking. Sprinkle on reserved bread crumbs. Bake for about 20 minutes in 400–425-degree oven. While baking, prepare:

6 lemon wedges
6 parsley sprigs
1½ cups Clarified Butter

Remove lobsters with tongs, place on platter, garnish with lemon wedges and parsley sprigs. Serve with about 1½ ounces heated clarified butter on the side for each person.

VARIATION: Allow large claws to remain on lobster and use ingredients listed, minus lobster meat, for stuffing.

HERBED SHRIMP SAUTÉ

2½ pounds shrimp, peeled and deveined (about 16–21 shrimp to the pound)
4 quarts water
2 tablespoons salt

Bring salted water to a fast boil and put in shrimp. As soon as water begins to boil again, remove at once to cold water and cool shrimp. Set aside.

Marinade

   6 tablespoons lemon juice
   2 cloves garlic, crushed
   ½ teaspoon chopped dill (or ¼ teaspoon dried)
   ½ teaspoon chopped tarragon (or ¼ teaspoon dried)
   Salt and fresh-ground pepper
   ½ cup oil

In large bowl mix marinade ingredients. Add shrimp, turn a few times to coat well with marinade. Cover and refrigerate for a few hours, turning once or twice.

To Cook

   6 tablespoons Clarified Butter
   1 tablespoon chopped chives
   1 tablespoon chopped parsley
   12 toast triangles
   Pinch paprika
   6 lemon wedges
   1½ cups Tartar Sauce

Remove shrimp from marinade and drain a few minutes. Heat the clarified butter in large skillet and when hot, sauté the shrimp, stirring frequently to heat and coat evenly. Sauté for about 5 minutes. During last minute stir in the chives and parsley. Pour onto warm platter and surround with toast triangles. Sprinkle on a pinch of paprika to color. Add lemon wedges and serve with a side dish of tartar sauce.

TARTAR SAUCE

   3–4 tablespoons finely chopped onion
   ¼ cup finely chopped kosher-type or dill pickle
   1 tablespoon capers, chopped
   1 tablespoon chopped parsley
   ¼ teaspoon sugar
   ½ teaspoon salt
   ¼ teaspoon fresh-ground pepper
   Juice of ½ lemon
   1½ cups Mayonnaise

Mix all ingredients together in a bowl. Cover and place in refrigerator. By keeping covered or placing in a screw-top jar, tartar sauce will keep for weeks in refrigerator. Makes about 2 cups.

SCALLOPS PARISIENNE

2½ pounds bay scallops (if using sea scallops, cut into halves or
    quarters depending on size)
4 tablespoons Clarified Butter
2 tablespoons chopped chives
2 tablespoons chopped parsley
1 tablespoon fresh lemon juice
Toast triangles
6 lemon wedges
Sprinkle of paprika
1½ cups Tartar Sauce

Dry scallops on a towel. Heat half of the butter in a heavy skillet. When hot, quickly sauté half the scallops. Remove from pan and set aside. Sauté the other half. When all scallops are done, add the remaining butter, chives, parsley, and lemon juice to the pan. When bubbling, pour all the scallops into the pan. Quickly coat scallops with hot butter sauce. Serve on warm platter flanked by toast triangles and a wedge of lemon. Serve tartar sauce in a side dish.

poultry

When it comes to entertaining, chicken is in a class by itself. It never lets you down. If dinner is delayed, chicken will wait patiently in the oven and do nothing but improve. It has an affinity for most herbs, sauces, and flavoring. Broiled, baked, fried, sautéed, roasted, or poached—it doesn't matter, the end result is delicious. What's more, everyone likes chicken and every country has different, interesting, and unusual ways of preparing it. For final charm, it is not only one of the best but also one of the least expensive entrees.

Our collection includes a few that take extra time to prepare. We include them because we think them especially good.

HERBED ROAST CHICKEN IN A BAG

2 roasting chickens, about 3–3½ pounds each
2 slices bacon
1 teaspoon dried sage
1 teaspoon dried rosemary
1 teaspoon dried tarragon
1 teaspoon salt
½ teaspoon fresh-ground pepper
⅔ cup oil
½ stick butter
2 brown paper bags, large enough to hold one chicken apiece

Inside each chicken put 1 slice of bacon (cut into small pieces). Mix herbs, salt, and pepper together, divide in two, and spoon into the chickens. Tie down the legs and wings. In a heavy skillet heat 4 tablespoons each of oil and butter and quickly brown chickens on all sides. Remove pan from heat and allow to cool.

Brush balance of oil on outside of paper bags. Place one chicken in each bag and tie tops of bags with string. Place in an oiled roasting pan and put into a preheated 350-degree oven for 15 minutes. After 15 minutes punch a few small holes in the bags to allow steam to escape. Continue roasting for about 45 minutes more. Remove from oven, allow a few minutes for juices to settle, then cut strings. Remove chickens to warm platter and pour juices into small pan to heat. To remove cavity juices, insert wooden spoon into cavity. Lift and tilt chicken over pan. After carving, pour hot juice over chickens. Sprinkle with parsley and serve. Any tart jelly goes well with this dish.

CHICKEN WITH FINE HERBS

3 1½–2-pound chickens, quartered
1 stick of butter, softened
2 tablespoons chopped parsley ⎫
2 tablespoons chopped chives ⎬ If using dried herbs,
2 tablespoons chopped tarragon ⎭ halve the quantity of each
1 teaspoon chopped oregano
Chopped parsley
½ cup stock or white wine

Cream together butter, parsley, chives, tarragon, and oregano. Gently lift up skin of chickens and spread herbed butter generously under the skin with your fingers. Pat down skin. Place chickens, skin side up, not touching, in a roasting pan and bake in a 425-degree oven for 30 minutes (or until nicely browned). Remove chickens to warm platter and keep hot. Add a little stock or wine to the pan and stir over high heat, scraping particles from bottom and sides. Add a little butter, blend well, and strain through a fine sieve over the chickens. Sprinkle with parsley and serve.

CHICKEN KELLEY-ROOS

6 boneless chicken breasts (6–8 ounces each, split in half)
1 teaspoon salt
½ teaspoon pepper   mixed together
½ teaspoon paprika
1 stick of butter
1 pound mushrooms, sliced
1 teaspoon dried tarragon (or 2 teaspoons fresh chopped)
2 tablespoons flour
½ cup sherry
1¼ cups chicken stock
2 15-ounce cans artichoke hearts, drained
Salt and fresh-ground pepper
2–3 teaspoons fresh chopped parsley

Dry chicken well and sprinkle with the mixture of salt, pepper, and paprika. Melt half the butter in a heavy skillet and when hot, sauté the chicken until a golden brown, being careful not to crowd the pan. When nicely browned, place chicken pieces in a large casserole and set aside. If needed, add balance of butter to same pan and sauté the mushrooms over medium heat for about 5 minutes. Add the tarragon and flour and stir well for a minute or two. Meanwhile heat sherry and chicken stock together and pour over the mushrooms. Stir gently as it comes to a boil and thickens, then simmer for 3–4 minutes. Check for seasoning and add more salt and pepper if necessary. Surround the chicken pieces with the artichokes and pour the mushroom sauce over the entire dish and cover. (At this point cooking may be stopped and the casserole cooled and stored in the refrigerator.)

Allow time for the casserole to come to room temperature (about an hour). Place in 350-degree oven and bake 40–45 minutes. Remove cover, sprinkle with chopped parsley, and serve at the table.

CHICKEN PAPRIKA

2 chickens, about 3½ pounds each, cut into serving pieces
Salt and fresh-ground pepper
3 tablespoons olive oil
6 tablespoons butter
2 large onions, finely chopped
3 tablespoons flour
2½ cups chicken stock, heated
1½ tablespoons paprika
2 tablespoons tomato paste
1 cup heavy cream
Juice of 1 lemon
2 tablespoons chopped parsley

Season chicken with salt and pepper. Heat oil and half of the butter in a skillet. Sauté chicken pieces until golden. Remove to covered roasting pan.

In the same skillet, heat the remaining butter and sauté onions until transparent (about 3 minutes). Off the stove, add the flour, stir until smooth, return to stove and cook for 3 minutes. Stir in hot chicken stock and slowly bring to a boil. Boil gently 3 minutes. Reduce heat and sprinkle in the paprika, then add tomato paste and blend well. Pour sauce over chickens, cover tightly, and bake in 350-degree oven for 30 minutes. Remove chicken to warm platter and keep hot. Add the cream, then lemon juice to the sauce and simmer for a few minutes. Check the seasoning, then spoon some of the sauce over the chicken. Garnish with parsley. Serve balance of sauce in gravy boat.

CHICKEN OREGANO

3 broiling chickens, 1½–1¾ pounds each, split in half
¾ cup olive oil
Juice of 2 lemons
Grated rind of 1 lemon
¼ cup white wine
¼ cup water
2 tablespoons oregano (dried)
1 tablespoon chopped parsley
1 teaspoon garlic powder
Salt and fresh-ground pepper
Sprigs of watercress or parsley (garnish)

Put chicken in bowl. Mix together oil, lemon juice and rind, wine, water, oregano, parsley, garlic powder, salt and pepper. Spoon over chicken pieces and let stand an hour or two, turning pieces occasionally. Remove chickens from marinade and place on cookie tin, place under broiler and broil about 15 minutes each side, basting occasionally with marinade, until golden brown. Remove to oven-proof copper pan or casserole, pour over some marinade and let bake in 325-degree oven 10–15 minutes, basting occasionally. Serve with a coating of hot marinade.

CHICKEN BREASTS WITH HAM

3 10-ounce breasts, boned, split in two, and skinned
⅓ cup flour, seasoned with salt and pepper
2 tablespoons olive oil
2 tablespoons butter
½ teaspoon dried sage
6 thin slices prosciutto or smoked ham
½ cup dry white wine
½ cup chicken stock
½ pound mushrooms, sliced
Salt and pepper to taste
Chopped parsley

Between sheets of wax paper pound chicken flat. Dip chicken in seasoned flour. Heat oil and butter in skillet and sauté chicken pieces on one side until golden. Turn chicken over and sprinkle a little sage on cooked side. Place ham on top. Sauté second side. Transfer chicken to ovenproof serving dish and set aside.

Pour wine into skillet and cook rapidly until reduced to one third of its original quantity. Strain into saucepan and add stock and mushrooms. Simmer 5–6 minutes. Pour over chicken. Cover tightly and bake in oven for 15 minutes at 300 degrees. Sprinkle with parsley and serve.

BREAST OF CHICKEN HONGROISE

    6 boneless chicken breasts (about 6–8 ounces each)
    2 tablespoons butter
    2 tablespoons finely chopped shallots (or onion)
    ½ cup dry white wine
    1½ tablespoons paprika
    ½ cup heavy cream
    ½ cup lean ham, cut into julienne strips
    Parsley sprigs

Sauce

    2 tablespoons butter
    2 tablespoons flour
    1½ cups chicken stock, hot
    Salt and fresh-ground pepper

In a heavy skillet melt butter and sauté chicken breasts until tender and a golden brown (about 15–20 minutes). *During this time make the sauce and put aside.* Remove chickens to a platter and keep warm. In the same skillet add shallots and wine, and cook until wine is reduced by about half. Stir in the paprika, then the sauce, and cook over low heat for 2 minutes. Strain into another pan. Add the cream and ham. Heat well but *do not boil.* Check for seasoning, then pour over chicken breasts. Garnish with parsley.

To Make the Sauce: Melt butter in a saucepan, stir in flour and cook over low heat for 3 minutes. Add the hot stock and bring to a boil, stirring constantly. Reduce heat and simmer for about 3 minutes. Check for seasoning.

CHICKEN SHERRY

⅔ cup flour
1 teaspoon salt
1 teaspoon garlic powder
1 teaspoon paprika
2 3-pound chickens, cut into serving pieces
2 tablespoons oil
1 stick butter
⅔ cup dry sherry
2 tablespoons soy sauce
3 tablespoons lemon juice
3 tablespoons finely chopped preserved ginger
2 tablespoons chopped parsley

Combine flour, salt, garlic powder, and paprika in a paper bag and shake chicken pieces lightly in bag to coat them. In a large skillet heat oil with ¼ stick of butter. When hot, brown chicken on all sides (adding extra butter if needed). Place chicken in covered baking pan and set aside.

In a saucepan combine remaining butter (¾ stick), sherry, soy sauce, lemon juice and ginger. Bring to a boil, stirring, and pour over chickens. Bake, covered, in a 350-degree oven for about 1 hour. Baste occasionally. Remove chicken to warmed ovenproof serving platter and hold in a slow oven (about 200 degrees). Pour 1 cup of water into the baking pan, bring to a boil, scrape pan well, and strain sauce into a pan. Pour some sauce over chicken; serve the balance in a gravy boat. Garnish with parsley.

CHICKEN MARSALA

2 chickens, about 3 pounds each, cut into serving pieces
1½ cups flour, seasoned with 1 teaspoon salt and ½ teaspoon pepper
4 ounces oil (olive or vegetable)
2 large onions, peeled, halved, and sliced lengthwise into ½ inch slices
2 green peppers, sliced the long way into ½ inch slices
½ pound mushrooms, cut into thick slices or quartered
2 cloves of garlic, minced
1 29-ounce can tomatoes

78

1 teaspoon sugar
1 tablespoon tomato paste
½ teaspoon ground oregano or marjoram
½ cup marsala wine
Salt and fresh-ground pepper to taste

Wash and dry chicken pieces and dredge in seasoned flour. Heat oil in skillet and, when hot, sauté chicken pieces a few at a time until golden brown. Remove to covered roasting pan. Set aside.

When all chicken is browned, sauté onions in same oil in skillet for about 5 minutes. Add green peppers and sauté 5 minutes more. Add mushrooms and sauté 5 minutes more. Now gently stir in minced garlic, tomatoes, sugar, tomato paste, oregano or marjoram, and then wine. Simmer 5 minutes. Check for seasoning.

Pour this sauce over chicken pieces in roasting pan. Cover roasting pan tightly and cook in oven at 350 degrees for about 30 minutes. Remove cover and cook for about 10–15 minutes more. Serve at table from warmed platter or casserole.

CHICKEN WITH WINE AND LEMON

½ cup dry white wine
2 2½-pound chickens, cut into serving pieces
6 tablespoons olive oil, or salad oil
2 cloves of garlic, minced
Grated rind and juice of 1 lemon
½ teaspoon ground thyme
Salt and fresh-ground pepper to taste
¼ pound butter
Chopped parsley

In a small pan boil the wine and reduce to half of its original quantity. In a large bowl blend together oil, garlic, lemon rind and juice, thyme, salt, pepper, and wine. Add the chickens and marinate in the refrigerator for at least 2 hours. Can be marinated overnight.

When ready to bake, butter an ovenproof dish or casserole and arrange chicken pieces in it. Pour the marinade over them, dot with butter, and bake in a 350-degree oven for about 1¼–1½ hours, or until tender, basting frequently. Sprinkle with parsley and serve.

BREAST OF CHICKEN FREDERICK

No question about it–this one is work. But if you want to make your reputation and have a uniquely delicious meal, roll up your sleeves and go to work.

1. 6 8-ounce boneless chicken breasts, cut in two

Marinade
> 3 tablespoons oil
> 3 tablespoons lemon juice
> 2 cloves of garlic, crushed
> 2 tablespoons grated Parmesan cheese or Romano
> ½ teaspoon ground oregano
> Salt and fresh-ground pepper

Combine the marinade ingredients in a large bowl. Mix thoroughly. Place chickens in marinade and refrigerate for 2–3 hours, turning occasionally. Remove chickens from marinade and drain for about 10 minutes.

2. 1½ cups flour
> 2 teaspoons paprika
> 1 teaspoon salt
> ½ teaspoon fresh-ground pepper
> 1 tablespoon grated cheese (Parmesan or Romano)
> ¼ cup oil
> ½ stick butter

In a large paper bag mix together flour, paprika, salt, pepper, and cheese. Pat chicken pieces dry and dredge a few at a time in the flour mixture. Heat oil and butter in a large skillet. When hot, sauté chicken breasts until a golden brown. Remove from heat and set aside. Save the fat in the skillet. Chicken may now be cooled and refrigerated for later use.

3. *Sauce*—Step 1
> 2½ cups chicken stock
> 1 bay leaf
> 1 onion, finely chopped
> ½ teaspoon salt

Combine above ingredients, bring to a boil, then simmer for about 15 minutes. Strain.

Sauce—Step 2
4 tablespoons butter
¼ cup finely chopped scallions (or onions)
½ cup finely chopped mushrooms
3 tablespoons flour
Salt and fresh-ground pepper

In a pan melt butter and sauté scallions about 3 minutes. Add mushrooms, sauté 3 minutes more. Stir in flour and cook 2 minutes. Add hot stock from Step 1, stirring, and bring to a boil. Taste and adjust seasoning, if necessary. (All of this can be done in the morning or even the day before.)

Grand Finale: About 40 minutes before serving time, reheat the skillet with the oil in which chickens were originally sautéed. The pan should be well-coated, but pour off some if it looks like too much. Place chicken breasts (*which have stood at room temperature for about ½ hour*) skin side up in a circle around the skillet, overlapping. Pour 3 tablespoons water into the center of the skillet, and cover tightly. Turn heat to medium low. The water will create steam. Let chickens steam for 20–25 minutes, then remove to warm serving platter, again overlapping. Ladle over some of the sauce, serve balance in a gravy boat. Garnish with sprigs of parsley (or chopped parsley). Buttered noodles are excellent with this dish.

ROAST DUCK

2 ducks, about 4 pounds each
½ cup chopped onion
½ cup chopped celery
½ teaspoon cinnamon
⅔ cup soy sauce
3 teaspoons sugar
⅓ cup sherry
1 tablespoon salt
⅓ cup honey
3 tablespoons red wine vinegar
Few sprigs watercress or parsley

Rinse inside of ducks. With sharp knife remove loose fat. Tie or truss neck of duck. In pan combine onion, celery, cinnamon, half of soy sauce, sugar, and sherry. Bring this mixture to a boil. Cool a little and pour half into cavity of each duck. Skewer together or sew up opening. Rub skin of ducks with salt. Place on rack in roasting pan and roast in a 475-degree oven for 30 minutes, pricking from time to time with a fork. Remove from oven and pour off fat. Combine remaining soy sauce with honey and vinegar in a small bowl. Brush this sauce over ducks. Turn oven down to 325 degrees and roast ducks for about 2½ hours, brushing with honey mixture every half hour. Remove ducks to warm platter. Keep warm. Pour off fat from roasting pan. Place pan on top of stove and add a cup of water. Bring to a boil, scraping particles from roasting pan. Set aside. Cut string ties or remove skewers from ducks. Place large spoon into cavity of each duck, lift duck up and tilt over pan so that the juices may run out. Strain combined juices into small pan and heat to simmer. Cut duck into serving pieces and arrange on warmed platter. Spoon over a little hot sauce. Garnish with watercress or parsley. Serve.

NOTE: If you find the ducks darkening too rapidly during roasting, cover with aluminum foil. Lift covering when basting.

meat

Meat is an important part of any meal and often takes a long time to prepare. However, it has fringe benefits second to none. Leftovers can make another family meal or be used for sandwiches. Or you can prepare a double quantity in the first place for such dishes as Beef Macconaise, remove half when not quite finished, freeze it, and be comfortably ahead for another dinner in the distant future.

Again, we have chosen those recipes for which we get the most requests.

STEAK MARIO

4½–5 pounds boneless sirloin steak, cut about 3 inches thick, trimmed. Have meat at room temperaure for about 1 hour before cooking.

Sauce Mario

½ cup dry red wine
1½ cups beef bouillon
Salt and fresh-ground pepper
1 clove garlic, minced
1 cup ketchup
¼ cup tomato paste
3 tablespoons Worcestershire sauce
2 tablespoons lemon juice
½ teaspoon sugar
1½ sticks butter
2 large onions, cut in ½-inch slices
3 green peppers, sliced as the onions
Chopped parsley

Place steak on broiling pan and set under preheated broiler as close as possible to the heat. Broil for 4–5 minutes on each side. Remove from broiler and set aside. In saucepan heat wine and bouillon until boiling, then add salt, pepper, garlic, ketchup, tomato paste, Worcestershire sauce, lemon juice, sugar, butter, onions, and green peppers. Cook for 10 minutes over medium heat.

Place steak on roasting pan, pour over about half the sauce, and bake in a 350-degree oven for 25–30 minutes. Steak should now be medium-rare. Remove steak to hot platter, pour any juices from roasting pan into remaining sauce, and heat thoroughly. Carve steak. Spoon on sauce. Garnish with parsley. Serve with gravy boat of additional sauce.

TOURNEDOS WITH SAUCE BÉARNAISE

Prepare Sauce Béarnaise ahead if preferable, and store in
    refrigerator
Prepare 6 white bread rounds, toasted or fried in oil or Clarified
    Butter until golden, drained on paper towels, and set aside
6 tournedos, about 1½ inches thick, weighing 7–8 ounces each,
    out of refrigerator for ½ hour
1 teaspoon of beef fat (trimmed from tournedos)
Chopped parsley

Trim the tournedos. In skillet melt fat until it just barely coats the base of the skillet. Place tournedos in very hot skillet (they should begin to sizzle immediately). Grill tournedos on both sides for a total time of about 9–10 minutes for medium-rare. Check by inserting a thin sharp knife into center of meat to see if cooked enough. On a warm platter arrange toast rounds and place one tournedo on each round. Spoon a dollop of sauce Béarnaise on each tournedo, sprinkle with parsley and serve.

SAUCE BÉARNAISE

This may be made in advance, poured into a bowl and refrigerated. Sauce Béarnaise has for its base Hollandaise sauce, so we are giving both here.

Blender Hollandaise
½ pound butter
4 egg yolks
2 tablespoons fresh lemon juice
¼ teaspoon salt
Pinch cayenne pepper

In a small pan heat butter to the point of bubbling, but do not let it burn. Into the blender container put egg yolks, lemon juice, salt, and cayenne pepper. Cover container and turn motor on low speed for 2 seconds (just long enough to blend the ingredients). Remove cover and pour in hot butter in a very slow, steady stream. When all butter has been added, turn off motor.

To Turn This Hollandaise into Sauce Béarnaise
2 tablespoons white wine
1 tablespoon tarragon vinegar
2 teaspoons fresh chopped tarragon (or ½ teaspoon dried)
2 teaspoons chopped shallots or onions
¼ teaspoon fresh-ground pepper
Hollandaise Sauce made as above, in blender

Combine wine, vinegar, tarragon, shallots, and pepper in a small saucepan, bring to a boil, and boil rapidly until almost all of the liquid has disappeared. Pour remaining concentrated brew into the Hollandaise sauce in the blender. Cover and blend on high speed for 6 seconds. Makes about 1 cup. Excellent on steaks, chops, and hamburgers.

SAUCE CHASSEUR

½ stick butter
1 large onion, cut in half and sliced
2 cups sliced mushrooms
1 cup dry red wine
1 teaspoon beef bouillon (or 1 bouillon cube)
2 teaspoons tomato paste
½ teaspoon Worcestershire sauce
Salt and fresh-ground pepper

Melt butter in a skillet. Add onion and sauté until golden, then add mushrooms and sauté together over low heat for about 10 minutes. Heat wine in a small pan and, when bubbling, add the bouillon. Stir the tomato paste into the wine-bouillon mixture and add to the onion-mushroom mixture. Add Worcestershire sauce, salt, and pepper. Simmer slowly, stirring as it thickens. Sauce is now ready to serve. If sauce is to be used at once it should be kept warm. If for later use, put in container, cover, and store in refrigerator. It will keep for days. Reheat slowly when ready to use.

SAUCE PROVENÇALE (for steaks and chops)

Sauce

1½ cups canned tomatoes (put through a strainer)
1 teaspoon sugar
½ cup dry red wine
1 teaspoon ground or chopped basil
½ teaspoon salt
⅛ teaspoon fresh-ground pepper

In a saucepan bring tomatoes to a slow simmer. Add the sugar, the wine, basil, salt, and pepper. Simmer slowly until sauce thickens. Set aside.

Garnish

4 tablespoons oil
1 medium onion, sliced into strips
1 large green pepper, seeded and cut into strips

½ medium-sized eggplant, peeled, cut into about ½ inch wide
    julienne strips, sprinkled with salt and allowed to stand 20
    minutes
1 pimiento, diced
12 black olives, pitted and halved

Heat oil in skillet. Sauté onion about three minutes in the oil. With
a slotted spoon remove onion and drain on paper towel. Sauté
green pepper in the same oil for 3–4 minutes. Drain on paper
towel. Sauté eggplant to golden. Drain. Place onion, pepper, eggplant, pimiento, and black olives on a large plate and gently mix
together.

When steaks are cooked and ready to serve, spoon 2 tablespoons of hot tomato sauce over the steak, and place some of the
vegetable garnish onto the sauce.

BEEF MACCONAISE

3½–4-pound eye of the round beef

Marinade

1 sliced onion
1 carrot, cut into chunks
1 garlic clove, crushed
2 tablespoons oil
6–8 crushed peppercorns
½ teaspoon salt
4 ounces dry red wine
6–8 crushed juniper berries (optional)

In a saucepan combine marinade ingredients. Simmer for 2 minutes, then allow to cool a little and pour over meat. Refrigerate
meat in marinade for 24–48 hours, turning meat once or twice.

To Cook

2 tablespoons oil
Beef, removed from marinade and dried on
    paper towels. Reserve Marinade.
1 clove garlic, crushed
1 stick celery, cut into chunks
½ cup beef stock (bouillon cube will do)
½ cup red wine

Heat oil in skillet and brown meat on all surfaces. Reduce heat, add garlic, celery, beef stock, and wine. Slowly bring to a boil. Add reserved marinade. Cover skillet and simmer for 2–2½ hours (or until meat is tender). Meat may be cooked on top of stove or in a 350-degree oven. During cooking turn meat once. While meat is cooking, prepare sauce.

Sauce

>   2 tablespoons butter
>   2 scallions, finely chopped
>   2 tablespoons flour
>   1 cup beef stock
>   6 ounces sliced mushrooms

Melt butter in frying pan and sauté scallions 3 or 4 minutes. Remove from heat, add flour, and mix. Return to stove and cook for 3 minutes. Stir in beef stock over low heat, then bring to a boil. Reduce heat, add mushrooms and simmer for 5 minutes. Set aside.

Remove cooked meat from skillet and keep warm. Skim off fat from juices in skillet. Strain juices into scallion-mushroom sauce. Stir gently. Bring to a boil. Check for seasoning. Keep warm and ready for serving. Carve meat into slices about ¼ inch thick. Lay slices neatly on warmed serving platter. Spoon sauce with mushrooms on top of meat in a line down the center. Sprinkle on a little chopped parsley for garnish. Serve balance of sauce in gravy boat.

NOTE: This dish may be done in advance, and will keep in refrigerator overnight. When ready to use, reheat sauce slowly. Slice meat and *reheat slowly* with a light covering of sauce.

This dish is enhanced by serving it with glazed onions on one side and glazed carrots on the other. (See Vegetables.)

ROULADE OF BEEF BURGUNDY

>   2½ pounds lean beef—such as bottom round, eye of the round, etc. Have butcher prepare 12 slices about ¼ inch thick and about 4 inches square. Slices should weigh around 3 ounces. Place meat between sheets of wax paper, and with cleaver or bottom of heavy skillet, pound meat until very thin, without breaking fibers of the meat.

Filling

    3 tablespoons butter
    1 medium onion, finely chopped
    ⅔ cup ground beef
    ⅔ cup finely chopped ham
    ⅔ cup bread crumbs
    1 large or 2 medium eggs, beaten
    Chopped parsley
    Salt and fresh-ground pepper

Melt butter in pan. Over medium heat sauté onion until golden, mix in the ground beef and ham, and cook for 6–8 minutes. Remove from flame, cool a little, add crumbs, and mix in egg and parsley. Season to taste. Put meat slices on work surface. Divide filling evenly and spoon into center of meat slices. Roll meat carefully over filling. Tie 1 inch from each end with string or secure with toothpicks.

To Cook

    4 tablespoons cooking oil
    1 cup flour

Heat oil in skillet. Roll meat lightly in flour and brown on all sides in the hot oil. Place meat in baking pan. Set aside.

Sauce

    1½ cups beef stock
    ½ cup dry red burgundy wine
    2 tablespoons tomato paste
    2 cloves garlic, minced
    Salt

Combine sauce ingredients and blend. Pour over meat, cover, and bake in a 350-degree oven for 1¼ hours (or until meat is tender). Turn once during cooking. Cook uncovered for last 15 minutes. Remove meat to a warm serving platter. Strain sauce into a pan. Check for seasoning. Pour some of the sauce over the meat, garnish with parsley and serve remaining sauce in gravy boat.

NOTE: Sliced mushrooms lightly sautéed in butter may be added to the sauce.

This dish can be done the day before and refrigerated. The flavor will improve with reheating.

BRISKET OF BEEF

2 tablespoons cooking oil
4 pounds lean brisket of beef
1 medium onion, sliced
1 stick celery, cut into chunks
Salt and fresh-ground pepper
1 clove garlic, finely chopped
1 8-ounce can tomatoes
½ teaspoon sugar
1 bay leaf
1½ cups dry red wine
Chopped parsley

Heat oil in a heavy skillet or Dutch oven. When hot, sear meat on all sides until well browned. Mix together and add to pot all remaining ingredients *except parsley*. Cover, and cook over medium heat 2½–3 hours, turning meat a few times during the cooking. When tender, remove meat to warm platter and set aside. Remove bay leaf from skillet and skim off the fat. Rub cooked vegetables and gravy juices through a strainer into a small pan. Check gravy for flavor. (At this point meat and gravy may be refrigerated for later use. Just as good, if not better, on the second day.)

When ready, heat gravy. Carve meat into ¼-inch slices. (Cool meat will slice better than hot.) Trim off most of the fat. Spoon some gravy onto serving platter. Place slices of meat over gravy. Spoon gravy on top of meat. Heat in a 250-degree oven about 15 minutes. Remove platter from oven, spoon on a little more hot gravy. Garnish with parsley and serve.

NOTE: Sliced mushrooms may be added to the gravy.

MEAT BALLS STROGANOFF

2 pounds ground beef
1 small onion, chopped fine
2 eggs, beaten
3–4 tablespoons milk
1½ cups fresh bread crumbs
Salt and fresh-ground pepper
2 tablespoons butter

Mix together beef, onion, eggs, milk, and bread crumbs. Season with salt and pepper. Moisten hands, then roll meat mixture lightly into balls about 1–1½ inches in diameter. Melt butter in skillet; when hot sauté the meat balls, turning them so that they brown evenly. Remove from skillet to warm bowl and set aside.

Sauce

   1½ cups beef stock
   3 tablespoons dry sherry
   1 tablespoon brandy
   1 cup sour cream
   Salt and fresh-ground pepper
   Paprika

Pour beef stock into skillet in which meat was cooked. Bring to a boil, scraping sides and bottom. Strain contents into a saucepan, add sherry and brandy, and bring to a boil. Reduce heat and add sour cream, blending well. Check the seasoning, then tip meat balls into the sauce and simmer, very slowly, for 15–20 minutes. *Do not boil sauce after sour cream has been added.* When ready to serve, pour onto a platter and sprinkle lightly with paprika.

VEAL PICCATA

   2 pounds veal scallops, pounded thin (12 pieces)
   ⅔ cup flour
   Salt and fresh-ground pepper
   3 tablespoons olive oil
   5 tablespoons butter
   3 tablespoons lemon juice
   2 tablespoons chopped parsley
   2 tablespoons chopped chives
   6 slices of lemon (seeds removed)

Wipe veal with paper towel. Mix together flour, salt, and pepper and dredge lightly. Heat oil and 3 tablespoons of butter in a heavy skillet. When butter stops foaming place a few veal pieces in the skillet, keeping them separate so that they do not touch. Sauté until golden brown—about 1½ minutes on each side. Remove veal from skillet and set aside. When all veal is sautéed, pour off the fat from the skillet, wipe skillet clean, and add the remaining 2 tablespoons of butter. When hot, return veal to skillet and turn pieces few times to heat evenly. Remove veal to warm platter, add lemon juice, parsley, and chives to skillet and heat rapidly while stirring. Spoon hot sauce over veal. Serve with a lemon slice on each piece.

VEAL BORGHESE

2 pounds veal scallops, cut into 12 pieces, pounded thin
½ cup flour
2 tablespoons olive oil
2 tablespoons butter
⅓ cup dry white wine
4 tablespoons butter
2 cups mushrooms, sliced thin
2 medium-sized tomatoes, peeled and diced
½ cup heavy cream
Salt and fresh-ground pepper
Chopped parsley

Dredge veal lightly in flour. Heat oil and the 2 tablespoons of butter in skillet and, when hot, sauté veal a few pieces at a time until golden brown on both sides. (Add a little more butter if needed.) Remove veal and set aside. When all veal is cooked, pour wine into the empty skillet, bring to a boil, and scrape the pan. Strain this juice into a bowl and set aside. In the same skillet melt remaining 4 tablespoons of butter and sauté mushrooms for 4–5 minutes. Add diced tomatoes and sauté 2–3 minutes more. Add heavy cream, and simmer a few minutes. Season carefully with salt and pepper. Add strained wine sauce to the skillet. Turn up heat but do not allow to boil. Put slices of veal in this sauce and turn veal a few times to coat evenly. Cook 3 minutes. Place portions of veal on warmed platter and spoon sauce on top. Garnish with chopped parsley and serve.

NOTE: This dish may be prepared in advance. Separate the sautéed veal and the sauce, and refrigerate. When ready to serve, allow veal to come to room temperature. Heat sauce, add veal, and serve as above.

VEAL ROLLATINE

2 pounds veal, cut into 12 thin scallops (of about 2½ ounces
   each), pounded thin
12 thin slices ham (prosciutto, spiced, or smoked)
6 slices Swiss, or Emmenthal cheese
1 10-ounce package frozen chopped spinach, defrosted
White string or toothpicks to tie veal rolls together
1 stick butter
2 cups stock (beef or chicken)
Salt and fresh-ground pepper
1 tablespoon chopped oregano
Chopped parsley

Wipe slices of veal dry. Cut or fold ham slices and set on veal to within ¼ inch of edge. Cut Swiss cheese into small julienne strips and place a few on each ham slice. Place 1 teaspoon chopped spinach on top of ham. Roll up veal scallops the long way and tie with string 1 inch from each end, or hold together with toothpicks. Dredge veal rolls in flour. Melt butter in skillet, and when hot, sauté veal rolls until golden brown. Remove veal rolls to roasting pan. Sprinkle 1 tablespoon of remaining flour into skillet, stir, and cook for 2 minutes. Pour in stock and, stirring, bring to boil to thicken. Season sauce with salt and pepper and pour over veal rolls. Sprinkle on oregano. Bake in a 350-degree oven for about 30 minutes. Arrange veal on warm platter and remove ties. Spoon sauce over veal and garnish with chopped parsley.

VEAL SCALLOPINI WITH MARSALA
   AND MUSHROOMS

Sauce

2 tablespoons butter
2 cups sliced mushrooms
1 tablespoon flour
1 cup beef or chicken stock
Salt and fresh-ground pepper to taste

In pan melt butter, add mushrooms, and sauté for about 5 minutes. Sprinkle in flour and cook for 3 minutes. Add stock and, stirring, bring to a boil. Season to taste. Set aside.

To Prepare Veal

2 pounds veal scallops, cut into 12 thin slices about 2½ ounces
    each, pounded thin
⅔ cup flour, seasoned with 1 teaspoon salt and ¼ teaspoon pepper
4 tablespoons butter
½ cup marsala wine
Juice of ½ lemon
6 lemon slices, seeds removed
Chopped parsley

Dredge veal in seasoned flour. Melt butter in skillet and, when butter has stopped foaming, add veal scallops a few at a time and sauté until golden brown. Add more butter if needed. As veal slices are done, remove to platter and set aside. Add wine and lemon juice to skillet and boil for a few seconds. Add mushroom-butter sauce. When warm, return veal to skillet. Cook over medium heat, turning a few times to evenly heat and coat. Place veal on warm platter and spoon on sauce. Garnish with lemon slices and parsley.

VEAL SCALLOPINI WITH PEPPERS AND TOMATOES

3 large green peppers
4 tablespoons olive oil
2 pounds veal scallops, pounded thin (12 pieces)
½ cup flour
1 14-ounce can tomatoes
½ teaspoon sugar
Salt and fresh-ground pepper
1 teaspoon oregano
Chopped parsley

Cut peppers into slices lengthwise. Heat oil in skillet and sauté peppers for 3–4 minutes. Remove peppers and set aside. Dredge veal in flour, and sauté in skillet a few pieces at a time, adding more oil if needed. Remove veal when golden to warm plate and set aside. Repeat until all veal is cooked. Return peppers to skillet, add tomatoes, sugar, salt, pepper, and oregano. Bring to a fast boil, then simmer. Return veal to skillet, turning frequently to heat. When thoroughly heated, serve covered with sauce. Garnish with parsley.

BUTTERFLY LAMB

1 leg of lamb, about 6 pounds. (Have butcher remove bone, spread meat open and trim rough edges. Save trimmings for other uses such as lamb stew or shish kabob.)

Marinade

1 large garlic clove, crushed
¾ cup oil
½ cup red wine
½ cup chopped onions
2 tablespoons Dijon, or 1 tablespoon dry mustard
2 teaspoons salt
1 teaspoon ground oregano
½ teaspoon ground basil
1 bay leaf
½ teaspoon fresh-ground pepper
½ teaspoon ground ginger

Combine marinade ingredients and simmer 10 minutes. Cool. Place lamb in a large bowl and pour marinade over lamb. Marinate in refrigerator for 24–48 hours, turning lamb a few times.

When ready to cook, remove lamb from marinade (reserve marinade) and put under broiler, fat side up, 3–4 inches from flame and broil about 10 minutes. Turn lamb over and broil about 8 minutes on second side. Set lamb in roasting pan and pour over reserved marinade. Roast in a 350-degree oven about 25–30 minutes. Lamb should be barely done, slightly pink in thick center of meat. Remove lamb and keep warm.

Sauce
> 2 tablespoons butter
> 1½ tablespoons flour
> ½ cup dry red wine, mixed with ½ cup water
> Sprigs of watercress or parsley

Melt butter in pan, stir in flour, and cook over medium heat for about 3 minutes. Set aside. Skim fat from roasting pan and set pan over heat on top of stove. Pour in wine-water mixture and cook until boiling while scraping bottom and sides of pan. Strain juices into butter-flour mixture. Cook for about 2 minutes. Season to taste.

Carve meat onto warm platter, spoon over some hot sauce, and garnish with watercress or parsley.

ROAST LEG OF LAMB DUXELLES

Duxelles Filling
> ½ stick butter
> ½ cup finely chopped onion
> 3 cups finely chopped mushrooms
> ½ cup white bread crumbs
> ½ teaspoon salt
> ¼ teaspoon fresh-ground pepper
> 2 tablespoons chopped parsley

Melt butter in pan over medium heat. Sauté chopped onion for about 10 minutes. Add mushrooms, and sauté for 10 minutes more, or until most of the liquid in pan has evaporated. Mix in bread crumbs, salt, and pepper. Add parsley. Blend well and set aside. (It may now be refrigerated for later use.)

To Prepare Lamb
> 1 leg lamb, about 6 pounds
> ½ teaspoon ground ginger
> 1 cup dry red wine
> 1 teaspoon garlic powder
> 2 tablespoons flour

Set oven at 425 degrees. Wipe lamb and rub with ground ginger. Pour on wine, sprinkle on garlic powder and flour. Insert meat thermometer, not touching bone. Roast for 20 minutes. Reduce heat to 300 degrees and roast for 2 hours more. While roasting, baste lamb a few times with drippings. (Pour 1 cup warm water over lamb if roasting pan is dry.) Remove lamb from oven when meat thermometer registers 140–150 degrees. Place lamb in clean pan or on a large platter. Cover with aluminum foil and place a towel over the foil.

Gravy

> 1½ cups chicken or beef stock
> ½ cup dry red wine
> ¼ teaspoon ground thyme
> 2 tablespoons mint sauce
> A few drops Kitchen Bouquet or caramel color
> Salt and fresh-ground pepper
> Chopped parsley

Pour fat from roasting pan and place pan on top of stove over high heat. Add stock and wine, and bring to a boil, scraping pan. Strain sauce into small pan. Add thyme, mint sauce, Kitchen Bouquet, salt, and pepper. Set aside and keep warm.

Remove lamb to carving board. Pour accumulated juices from lamb into gravy. Spoon about ½ cup gravy over bottom of copper server or ovenproof serving dish. Carve lamb into 12 thin slices. Place 6 largest on bottom of serving dish. Spread duxelles over each slice. Top with remaining lamb slices. Spoon over a little gravy. If not ready to serve, cover with aluminum foil. (It may now be refrigerated until ready for use.)

When ready, remove from refrigerator and allow meat to stand at room temperature for about an hour. Preheat oven to 300 degrees. Place covered lamb in oven for about 15 minutes. Remove foil, raise heat to 400 degrees, and heat about 5 minutes more. Have hot gravy ready. Spoon on a little more hot gravy. Garnish with chopped parsley and serve.

HERBED ROAST LEG OF LAMB

Leg of lamb, about 6 pounds
½ teaspoon ground marjoram
½ teaspoon thyme
½ teaspoon ground rosemary
¼ teaspoon garlic salt or garlic powder
½ bottle (about 3 ounces) mint sauce, mixed with ½ cup water
2 tablespoons flour
1 onion, sliced
1 carrot, sliced
1 stick celery, sliced
1 cup dry red wine

Place lamb on roasting pan. Mix together marjoram, thyme, rosemary, and garlic, and rub on lamb. Pour on half the mint sauce-water mixture. Sprinkle on flour. Place in a 350-degree oven and roast for about 30 minutes, then pour on the balance of mint sauce-water mixture. Roast 30 minutes more. Remove lamb to platter and lower oven heat to 300 degrees. Place onion, carrot, and celery slices on bottom of roasting pan and place lamb on top of vegetables. Insert meat thermometer, not touching bone. Pour on red wine. Return to oven and roast for about 1 hour and 15 minutes, basting a few times. Remove lamb when it is just done. (Meat thermometer should register 140–150 degrees, or a thin-bladed knife inserted into thick part of lamb will cause juices to run slightly on the pink side.) Remove lamb to warm platter and cover with aluminun foil and a towel.

Pour off fat from roasting pan. Place pan on top of stove, add ½ cup water or red wine. Bring to a boil and scrape pan thoroughly. Strain juices into a small saucepan.

Gravy

2 tablespoons butter
1 tablespoon flour
1 bouillon cube dissolved in ⅔ cup boiling water
Salt and fresh-ground pepper
Chopped parsley

Melt butter, stir in flour, and cook 2 minutes. Pour in juices from pan, add bouillon, and bring to a boil to thicken. Season to taste and keep warm. If not carving at the table, slice lamb into fairly thin slices, arrange on platter, and spoon on hot gravy. Garnish with parsley and serve with remaining gravy in gravy boat.

ROAST LOIN OF PORK

Pork loin, about 5 pounds. Have butcher remove chine bone, but leave rib bones in
Salt and fresh-ground pepper
½ teaspoon garlic powder
½ teaspoon ground rosemary
1 medium onion, sliced
1 stick celery
1 carrot, sliced
1½ cups beef or chicken stock
½ cup dry white wine
3 tablespoons fat from roast
1½ tablespoons flour
Chopped parsley

Rub pork with mixture of salt, pepper, garlic powder, and rosemary. Place in roasting pan in a 350-degree oven. Roast for 1 hour fat side up. Remove pork from pan, pour off fat, place onion, celery, and carrot in pan and place pork over vegetables. Continue roasting for about 1¾ hours longer. When meat is done, remove from roasting pan, cover meat, and keep warm. Drain fat from pan, *saving 3 tablespoonfuls*. Place roasting pan on top of stove, add stock and wine, and bring to a boil, scraping pan to loosen bits. Set aside. In small pan heat reserved 3 tablespoons of fat. Add flour. Cook over medium heat 3–4 minutes. Strain in juices from roasting pan. Bring to a boil, stirring, then simmer a few minutes. Season to taste and keep warm.

Remove roast to warm platter and slice between ribs, allowing 1 rib and 1 thin slice per portion. Add parsley to gravy and spoon over meat.

NOTE: Pork when done should be crisp on the outside and of a deep golden color. The inside should be white, not pink. To make certain, cut into thick section of meat. If meat is pink, turn up heat to 400 degrees and roast about 15 minutes more.

HAM VÉRONIQUE

Smoked ham (boneless about 4–4½ pounds, with bone about 6–7 pounds)

Bouquet garni (parsley sprigs, bay leaf, tarragon, and crushed peppercorns placed in a small cheesecloth bag and tied with string)

Poach ham in water to cover by first boiling, then allowing to simmer for about 15 minutes. Check water. If it is very salty, pour off and poach again with fresh water. Add bouquet garni to poaching water and simmer ham for about 2 hours.

Sauce

¾ cup dry white wine
2 tablespoons finely chopped onion
3 egg yolks
1 stick butter, softened
3 tablespoons flour
2 cups stock (chicken or stock from cooked ham)
½ cup heavy cream
6 ounces seedless white grapes
Salt and fresh-ground pepper to taste
Chopped parsley for garnish

In a saucepan bring wine to boil and reduce to about ½ cup. Add onion to wine. Set aside. In a bowl, set in warm water, beat egg yolks until lemon color. Add strained warm wine slowly, beating constantly. Add 1 tablespoon softened butter and mix in. Then slowly whisk in 3 more tablespoons of butter. Season to taste with salt and pepper. Set aside.

In a small skillet melt the other 4 tablespoons of butter, stir in flour and cook over medium heat for 3 minutes. Remove from heat, add hot stock, whisking to a smooth paste. Now bring the two sauces together and simmer. (The sauce should be smooth with the texture of heavy cream. If sauce is not smooth, put through strainer.)

At this point cooking may be stopped. Everything may be placed in refrigerator and held until ready.

When ready, heat ham once again in hot stock. Slowly reheat sauce, add cream, and simmer, but do not boil. Slice ham onto warmed platter. Add grapes to sauce and spoon sauce over ham slices. Serve at once, sprinkled with chopped parsley. Serve remaining sauce in gravy boat.

STUFFED FILLET OF PORK

> 3 pork tenderloin fillets, about 1–1¼ pounds each. Have butcher butterfly pork and flatten.

Filling

> 4 ounces ground pork (or veal)
> 4 ounces ground sausage meat
> 4 ounces ground ham
> 4 tablespoons white bread crumbs
> 1 teaspoon mixed herbs (chopped parsley, chives, and sage)
> Grated rind and juice of 1 lemon
> 1 egg, beaten
> ½ teaspoon salt
> ¼ teaspoon fresh-ground pepper

Place pork fillets on work surface, opened like pages of a book. Mix all filling ingredients together. Place filling on one side of fillet. Gently close fillet and sew or truss edges to seal in filling. Mold into shape of submarine.

To Cook

> ½ stick softened butter
> ½ cup dry white wine
> ⅔ cup chicken or beef stock
> ¼ cup sherry wine
> Chopped parsley

Place fillets on roasting pan. Brush thoroughly with softened butter. Pour on white wine and stock. Roast in a 400-degree oven, basting frequently. When fillets are well browned, remove from oven. Remove trussing. Cut, diagonally, into slices about 1½ inches thick. Arrange on platter. Strain juices from roasting pan into small pan. Bring to boil. In separate pan heat sherry, ignite with a match and pour into gravy. Stir and pour some gravy over fillets. Garnish with parsley. Serve remaining hot gravy in a gravy boat.

vegetables

There is no substitute for garden-fresh vegetables, especially if they come out of your very own vegetable patch. More and more of us are growing our own, experimenting with ever-increasing varieties, and marveling at the wonders we too can produce.

The exception is potatoes, which take up a lot of space in the garden and are every bit as good if purchased at the grocery store. In fact they will keep perfectly for months. With the notable exception of the tiny new ones that, boiled until tender, lightly salted, and shaken in a mixture of melted butter, snipped dill, and chopped parsley, are food for the gods.

If you haven't a garden, or nearby farms, or even a store specializing in fresh vegetables, then by all means use frozen. They are a very good second-best.

BAKED ASPARAGUS SPEARS

2 pounds fresh asparagus
6–8 tablespoons butter
1 teaspoon salt
¼ teaspoon fresh-ground pepper

Trim asparagus spears to uniform size of about 5 inches in length. Scrape ends and rinse spears in cold water. Butter a baking dish large enough to hold asparagus in two layers. Dot generously with butter and add salt and pepper. Cover tightly with aluminum foil and bake in a 300-degree oven for about 30 minutes or until tender.

GREEN BEAN CASSEROLE

1½ pounds fresh green beans
2–3 tablespoons fresh bread crumbs
½ stick butter
1 large garlic clove, minced
Salt and fresh-ground pepper
½ cup chopped parsley
1 cup sour cream

Put beans in a saucepan in cold, salted water to cover. Bring to a boil, then simmer, uncovered, for 15–20 minutes, or until tender. Drain well. Sauté bread crumbs in butter until lightly browned. Stir in garlic, salt, pepper, and parsley. Add beans to this mixture, stir gently, and tip into casserole. Pour sour cream over top and bake casserole in a 350-degree oven for 20 minutes. Serve hot.

GREEN BEANS AND MUSHROOMS

2 tablespoons butter
1 cup sliced mushrooms
4 cups cooked green beans
1 cup sour cream
Salt and fresh-ground pepper
1 tablespoon chopped parsley

Melt butter and sauté mushrooms 3–4 minutes over medium heat. Add green beans and sour cream and mix well. Season to taste with salt and pepper. Sprinkle with parsley and serve.

CABBAGE AND APPLES CORDON BLEU

2–2½ pounds cabbage (red or white)
½ stick butter
1 medium onion, sliced
2–3 tart apples
3 tablespoons wine vinegar
3 tablespoons water
1 tablespoon sugar
Salt and fresh-ground pepper
2 tablespoons butter, blended with 1 tablespoon flour

Quarter cabbage, cut out stalks, and shred very fine. Blanch in boiling water for about 1 minute and drain. Set aside. Melt butter in a saucepan. Add onion and cook over medium heat until soft. Peel, core, and slice apples and add to onion. Cook over medium heat 3–4 minutes. Turn out into a bowl. Place half the blanched cabbage into saucepan. Add a layer of apple mixture. Repeat both. Sprinkle vinegar, water, sugar, and seasoning over the top. Cover pan with buttered paper and place a lid over the paper. Cook over low heat for about 1½ hours, turning gently once or twice. It should be tender. If not, cook a little longer. Stir in kneaded butter-flour. Raise heat for a minute or two, stirring gently as flour mixture thickens. Turn down heat and cook over low heat a few minutes more. Check for seasoning. Serve.

NOTE: This dish may be varied slightly by adding some cara-way seeds. It will keep well in the refrigerator. When ready to serve, warm it very slowly, adding a few tablespoons of water if necessary.

GLAZED CARROTS

1 package carrots
2 tablespoons butter
2 teaspoons sugar
Salt
Chopped parsley

Peel carrots with vegetable parer. Cut into pieces 1¼–1½ inches long and round cut edges with parer. Put in saucepan, with just enough water to cover, add butter, sugar, and salt. Boil, covered, over medium heat for 15 minutes. Remove cover and turn up heat as high as possible. In about 15 minutes most liquid will have evaporated and butter and sugar will form a glaze. Watch carefully during this time to avoid scorching. Reduce heat. Shake pan so that all the carrots will be coated with glaze. If made ahead, reheat in the top of a double boiler or in an ovenproof dish in the oven. Carrots will be a bright orange. Sprinkle with parsley before serving.

CAULIFLOWER GRATINÉ

2 medium-sized cauliflower heads

Cut cauliflower into flowerets by first quartering, then cutting out thick stems, and trimming off leaves. Place flowerets in bowl of salted cold water and let stand for about 30 minutes. Remove flowerets and put into a pot of boiling water containing 1 tablespoon salt. Bring water back to boil and cook for about 15 minutes (or until tender). Set aside.

Sauce Gratiné

4 tablespoons butter
2 tablespoons flour
1¼ cups heated milk
Salt and fresh-ground pepper
Pinch nutmeg
3 tablespoons grated Gruyère cheese
3 tablespoons grated Parmesan cheese
3 tablespoons white bread crumbs

Melt butter in pan. Stir in flour and cook over medium heat 2 minutes. Add milk and bring to a boil, stirring constantly. Add salt, pepper, nutmeg, and Gruyère cheese. Butter the inside of a bowl just large enough to hold cauliflower. Spoon half of the sauce into the bowl. Break cauliflower into smaller flowerets and press lightly into bowl until filled. Cover with plate and warm in a 300-degree oven for about 20 minutes. Remove bowl from oven.

Place ovenproof dish over bowl and flip bowl over, releasing mound of cauliflower onto dish. Mix Parmesan cheese and bread crumbs with balance of sauce and ladle over cauliflower. Bake in 400-degree oven until brown, about 15–20 minutes. Cut into wedges at table.

CUCUMBERS IN DILLED NOISETTE BUTTER

3 cucumbers (select long, firm ones)
6 tablespoons butter
Juice of ½ lemon
1 teaspoon dill weed
Salt and fresh-ground pepper

Peel cucumbers, split in two lengthwise, and cut each half into bite-sized pieces. Cook in boiling, salted water for about 5 minutes (or until just tender). Pour off the water. In another pan, over low heat, melt butter, add lemon juice, and dill weed. Pour over cucumbers and mix gently. Season to taste. Serve hot.

LEEKS AU GRATIN

2 bunches leeks
Boiling water to cover
1 teaspoon salt
1 ounce butter
½ teaspoon pepper
½ cup grated Cheddar and Parmesan cheese mixed

Wash, trim and split leeks lengthwise, eliminating most of the green parts. Cook in boiling salted water about 15 minutes. Drain.

Arrange on buttered baking dish. Sprinkle with the pepper and the cheese. Heat under broiler until cheese is melted.

ONION, MUSHROOM, AND GREEN PEPPER SAUTÉ

3 large onions
4 tablespoons butter
1 large or 2 small green peppers
1 pound mushrooms
Salt and fresh-ground pepper
1 teaspoon lemon juice
Chopped parsley

Peel onions, cut in half, and cut lengthwise into thin slices. Do the same with the green peppers. Melt butter in skillet and sauté onions and peppers until onions are transparent. Wash and trim mushrooms; slice larger ones and use small ones whole. Add mushrooms to pan containing onions and peppers, stir, cover, and cook over low heat for about 10 minutes. Season to taste with salt and pepper and add lemon juice. Stir gently, pour into warm serving dish, and sprinkle with parsley.

GLAZED ONIONS

1½ pounds small white onions
2 tablespoons butter
1 tablespoon vegetable oil
1 teaspoon salt
2 tablespoons sugar

Place onions in cold water, bring to a boil, and boil for 1 minute. Remove from stove, tip into colander and shake under running cold water. The onions will now peel easily. In a large skillet heat together butter and oil. Add onions. Sprinkle with salt and sugar and shake pan until onions are well coated. Cook over *very low* heat, uncovered, occasionally turning, until onions are a nut-brown color. (May require an hour.) Can be reheated in an ovenproof dish in a medium oven.

NOTE: Onions can be bought in cans or jars and require only 10–15 minutes of glazing, using the same ingredients and cooking over medium heat. However, as these onions are preboiled, they are soft and require very gentle turning during glazing.

PEAS ELIZABETH

4 cups shelled peas
½ cup boiling water
4 scallions, chopped or thinly sliced
1 cup shredded lettuce
1 teaspoon chervil
1 teaspoon sugar
2 tablespoons butter
Salt and fresh-ground pepper

Place peas in saucepan. Pour on boiling water and cook, covered, about 5 minutes. Add all remaining ingredients, and cook, uncovered, over medium heat for about 5 minutes more (or until barely tender). Check for seasoning. Serve.

NOTE: Frozen peas may also be used.

SNOW PEAS—otherwise known as Edible Pod Peas

4 whole scallions, thinly sliced
4 tablespoons butter
½ cup sliced water chestnuts
1 cup sliced mushrooms
1¼–1½ pounds snow peas
½ cup chicken broth
1 teaspoon cornstarch dissolved in 2 tablespoons cold chicken
    broth
1 tablespoon soy sauce
Salt and fresh-ground pepper to taste

Sauté scallions in 2 tablespoons butter until softened. Add water chestnuts and cook 5 minutes over low heat. Set aside.

In a separate pan melt remaining 2 tablespoons butter and sauté mushrooms for 3 minutes. Combine mushrooms and scallion mixture. Add snow peas, chicken stock (with cornstarch), and soy sauce. Bring to a boil and simmer 2 minutes. Season to taste. Serve hot.

MINTED PEAS

We admit that shelling peas is a chore, but they are in season such a short time and so delicious that if you have willing helpers in the shelling department they are worth a little extra effort.

3 cups shelled fresh peas
½ cup boiling water
1 teaspoon chervil (optional)
1 teaspoon sugar
2 tablespoons butter
1 teaspoon salt
2–3 tablespoons chopped fresh mint

Cover peas with the boiling water, add the remaining ingredients (except mint), and cook until barely tender (about 5 minutes). Sprinkle with mint and serve.

BAKED STUFFED POTATOES

6 medium-sized Idaho potatoes
2 tablespoons butter
1 egg
3 tablespoons cream or milk
Pinch of ground nutmeg
Salt and fresh-ground pepper to taste
Chopped parsley

Wash and dry potatoes. Prick ends with a fork, put in a 375-degree oven, and bake for 1 hour (or until thoroughly done). Cut in two the long way and scoop out the warm pulp into a bowl. Lightly salt the potato shells. Mash the potatoes by hand or in the mixer. Add butter, egg, cream, nutmeg, salt, pepper, and chives. Mix thoroughly, taste, and adjust seasoning. Fill the potato shells, pressing top down lightly with the back of a fork. Potatoes may now be refrigerated. (They may also be frozen, uncovered, until firm, then put into bags and tied.) When ready to serve unfrozen ones, dot with butter and bake in a 300-degree oven for 20–25 minutes. Sprinkle with parsley.

NOTE: For variety add 2–3 tablespoons grated Cheddar cheese to the mashed-potato mixture.

PAN POTATOES

2 pounds medium-sized potatoes
½ stick butter
Salt and fresh-ground pepper

Peel potatoes, slice thin, and dry well on paper towels. Rub half the butter around sides and bottom of frying pan. Arrange the best, most even potato slices tightly overlapping on bottom of pan. Season well, dot with butter, and layer remaining potatoes, seasoning each layer with salt, pepper, and butter. Fill to even top. Cover with buttered, fitted paper, and then a lid. Cook over low heat on top of stove for 20 minutes. Then place in a 350-degree oven for another 20 minutes. Remove cover and bake 10 minutes more or until potatoes are done. Remove from oven. Run a knife around the edge of the pan, then flip over onto a heated platter so that the browned bottom is on top.

POTATOES MAÎTRE D'HÔTEL

2–2½ pounds uniform medium-sized new potatoes
Boiling water to cover
1 tablespoon salt

Peel and wash potatoes and place in boiling salted water. Cover and cook for 25–30 minutes or until just done. Drain and shake in uncovered pan over low heat to dry the potatoes. Set aside.

Sauce

4 tablespoons melted butter
Salt and fresh-ground pepper
1 tablespoon lemon juice
¼ teaspoon paprika
2 tablespoons fresh chopped parsley

Pour melted butter over potatoes in the pan. Shake pan over low heat to coat potatoes with butter. Season with salt and pepper. Add lemon juice. Shake potatoes a few times more. Sprinkle on paprika, then chopped parsley. Serve.

NEW ENGLAND HASHED BROWN POTATOES

This recipe will work equally well for day-old baked potatoes or for fresh-baked ones.

5–6 cups cold baked potatoes, skin removed, and diced
1 medium onion, chopped fine
3 tablespoons oil
2 tablespoons butter
Salt and fresh-ground pepper
½ cup finely chopped green pepper (optional)

Heat oil and butter in skillet and sauté onions until transparent. Add the diced potatoes. Turn up heat and sauté potatoes, stirring occasionally, until they begin to brown. Reduce heat to medium. Season to taste. Add the green pepper. Cook a few minutes more. Turn onto warmed platter and serve.

NOTE: If done in advance this dish will keep well in a 250-degree oven for about an hour.

POTATO PANCAKES

1½ pounds potatoes, peeled
Juice of ½ lemon
1 medium onion, grated
2 eggs
1 cup matzoh meal
Salt and fresh-ground pepper
1½ cups oil

In a large bowl grate the potatoes. Add lemon juice and onion. Beat in the eggs. Add 1 cup matzoh meal. The mixture should now be quite moist but not liquid. Add more matzoh meal if necessary. Season with salt and pepper.

Heat oil in a heavy skillet until hot. Gently place heaping tablespoonfuls of the mixture into the hot oil. It should begin to sizzle at once. If not, increase heat before adding more mixture. Place as many spoonfuls as possible into the oil without crowding the pan. To check if done—gently lift bottom edge of pancake to see if color is golden. When golden turn pancake over with tongs or two forks. When completely golden brown, pancakes are done. Remove finished pancakes to warmed platter. Cover with paper towel. Place in a 150–200-degree oven to keep warm. Serve when all pancakes are cooked. This recipe should make about 12 pancakes.

This dish goes well with pot roast, sauerbraten, and other meat dishes. It is also delicious with applesauce or sour cream.

NOTE: If matzoh meal is unavailable—sift together 4 tablespoons all-purpose flour with 4 tablespoons bread crumbs and ¼ teaspoon baking powder, and use in place of matzoh meal.

MASHED POTATOES and POMMES MOUSSELINE

Mashed potatoes and pommes mousseline differ from each other mainly in texture. Both are prepared in much the same manner, but the finished texture of pommes mousseline is creamy and light, while mashed potatoes are of a stiffer consistency.

Mashed Potatoes

2 pounds potatoes
3 tablespoons butter
¾ cup boiling milk
Salt and pepper

Peel potatoes and place in lightly salted cold water. Allow to stand about ½ hour. Then bring to a boil and boil steadily uncovered until done. Pour off the water and place pan on stove or in oven over low heat for a few minutes to evaporate most of the excess moisture. (It's important that potatoes be kept hot during the following steps. Have potato ricer, or metal strainer, and warmed bowl ready at hand.) Push potatoes through ricer or strainer into warmed bowl, then back into hot pan in which potatoes were cooked. Add a little hot milk and some of the seasoning, and beat with a wooden spoon. By degrees add butter and hot milk and keep beating. Add seasoning to taste. Serve.

NOTE: If potatoes are to be served at a later time, smooth the top of the potatoes with the back of a spoon; pour on ¼ cup hot milk and put pan in about 150-degree oven. It will keep well for about 1½ hours. When ready to serve, beat once again with wooden spoon.

Pommes Mousseline

2 pounds potatoes
3 tablespoons butter
1½–2 cups boiling milk
Pinch of ground nutmeg
Salt and pepper to taste

Follow same procedure as for mashed potatoes, adding pinch of nutmeg after mashing. By using the extra milk and beating well the final texture is creamier.

Further flavor interest may be created by blending into the finished potatoes any of the following:

Grated orange peel
Finely chopped chives
Finely chopped green scallion tops
Finely chopped watercress
Finely chopped parsley
Finely chopped crisp bacon
Fresh grated Cheddar cheese

NOTE: An electric hand held beater can be used effectively in place of a wooden spoon in either recipe.

POTATOES REPUCCI

2–2½ pounds potatoes
½ cup grated Parmesan cheese
½ cup light cream
Salt and fresh-ground pepper
4 tablespoons butter
½ cup grated Cheddar cheese
Pinch paprika

Peel potatoes and boil until done. While still hot, chop potatoes into uneven-sized pieces and place in ovenproof dish or pan. Add Parmesan cheese, cream, salt and pepper to taste, and butter, cut into small pieces. Mix gently and smooth top until fairly level. Bake in a 300-degree preheated oven for 10 minutes. Remove from oven, sprinkle on the Cheddar cheese, return to oven and bake 10 minutes more at 300 degrees until cheese melts on top. Sprinkle with paprika.

ROAST POTATO CHIPS

6–8 Idaho potatoes
½ of a lemon
1 stick melted butter
Salt and fresh-ground pepper
½ teaspoon paprika

Peel potatoes and slice into rounds ⅛ inch thick. Put in bowl of ice water. Squeeze lemon juice over potatoes and drop lemon into bowl. Put bowl in refrigerator for a few hours. Drain potatoes and dry on paper towels. Arrange on well-buttered large baking tin, and brush additional butter over the potatoes. Season lightly with salt, pepper, and paprika. Cover with foil and bake in a 350-degree oven for about 30 minutes. Remove foil and bake uncovered for 20–30 minutes more, turning potatoes from time to time, until chips are browned and crisp.

POTATOES DAUPHINE

4 tablespoons butter
½ teaspoon garlic powder
1½–2 pounds Idaho potatoes
Salt and fresh-ground pepper
½ teaspoon nutmeg
2 eggs
4 tablespoons milk
4 tablespoons grated Cheddar cheese

Butter an ovenproof dish or baking pan. Peel potatoes and cut into thin, round slices. Set half the potatoes in pan, season with salt, pepper, garlic powder, and a little nutmeg. Cover with remaining potatoes, season again with salt, pepper, garlic powder, and nutmeg. Beat eggs, add milk, and beat together. Strain mixture over the potatoes. Sprinkle grated Cheddar cheese over the top. Place dish in a pan of water (coming halfway up) in oven and bake at 325 degrees for about an hour (or until potatoes are soft).

This dish may be set aside to cool or refrigerate. When ready to use, cover tightly with aluminum foil, and heat in a 325-degree oven for about 30 minutes. Just before serving, run under broiler for a minute to brown the top.

RATATOUILLE

1½ pounds eggplant, peeled and cut into ¾-inch dice
1 pound zucchini, washed and cut into slices ½ inch thick,
    unpeeled
2–3 tablespoons salt
½ cup oil (olive oil preferred)
2 tablespoons olive oil (if needed)
2 large onions, sliced into long strips
2 green peppers, sliced into strips
1 pound tomatoes, peeled, some of the juice squeezed out,
    then diced
1 tablespoon chopped parsley
1 teaspoon chopped oregano
½ teaspoon chopped basil
1 teaspoon sugar
2 garlic cloves, minced
Salt and fresh-ground pepper

Spread diced eggplant and sliced zucchini on large platter. Sprinkle with salt and allow to stand for about ½ hour. The salt will cause the vegetables to release moisture and any bitter taste. Pat dry with paper toweling before using.

Heat oil in large skillet. Sauté the eggplant and zucchini until golden. Do not crowd skillet. As soon as vegetables are golden, remove to large saucepan.

In same skillet sauté the onions and peppers until onions become transparent. Add onions and peppers mixture to eggplant, plus tomatoes, parsley, oregano, basil, sugar, and garlic. Season to taste. (Dish may now be refrigerated until needed.) When ready, heat ratatouille slowly, stirring gently a few times. Cook only until hot. By not overcooking, this dish retains much of its original color. Check for seasoning. Serve hot.

To Skin Tomatoes: Place tomatoes in bowl and pour boiling water over them for a few seconds, then dip tomatoes into cold water. Skin will now peel off with a sharp stainless steel vegetable knife.

SPINACH MARGUERITE

3 packages frozen chopped spinach
½ cup chicken stock
2 tablespoons butter
1 medium onion, finely chopped
4 tablespoons sour cream
¼ teaspoon grated nutmeg
Salt and fresh-ground pepper
2 hard-cooked eggs, sliced
Chopped parsley

Cook spinach with chicken stock until just cooked. Drain. Melt butter in skillet and sauté onion until golden. Add onion, cream, nutmeg, salt, and pepper to spinach and place in ovenproof dish. Cover with buttered paper and cook in a 325-degree oven for 15–20 minutes. Decorate with slices of egg (or grated egg). Sprinkle with parsley and serve.

STEAMED PATTY PAN SQUASH

2 pound squash—the small ones are tastiest
½ cup chicken stock
½ stick butter
Salt and fresh-ground pepper
Chopped parsley

Wash squash and place in pan with chicken stock. Cover tightly. Bring to a boil, then reduce heat to steam slowly for 10–15 minutes. With fork check squash. It should be tender, yet fairly firm. Pour off stock, add butter and seasoning. Coat squash well. Sprinkle on parsley and serve.

NOTE: If squash are of uneven size, cut the larger ones in half before cooking.

Patty pan squash is also known as Bush Scallop squash.

BROILED TOMATOES

6 medium-sized firm tomatoes
4 tablespoons fresh bread crumbs
½ teaspoon ground oregano

¼ teaspoon sugar
1 teaspoon salt
½ teaspoon fresh-ground pepper
2 tablespoons butter, melted
2 strips bacon, cut in thirds

Cut tops from tomatoes. Scoop out 1 tablespoon of tomato pulp from each tomato. Place pulp in a bowl and mix with bread crumbs, oregano, sugar, salt, pepper, and melted butter. Stuff tomatoes with this mixture. Bake in a 325-degree oven for about 15 minutes. Place a piece of bacon on top of each tomato and broil until bacon is crisp.

BAKED ZUCCHINI

6 zucchini, about 4–6 ounces each
1 teaspoon salt
2–3 shallots
½ cup bread crumbs
6 tablespoons butter
Salt and fresh-ground pepper
6 strips bacon

Split unpeeled zucchini lengthwise and parboil halves for about 2 minutes in boiling salted water. Drain, and place skin side down in a shallow baking dish. Mince the shallots and scatter over the zucchini. Sprinkle on bread crumbs, and add small dots of butter. Season lightly. Bake in a 325-degree oven 15 minutes. Remove from oven. Place half strips of bacon over zucchini. Bake 15 minutes more, until zucchini is tender and bacon is crisp.

ZUCCHINI SAUTÉ

2 pounds small zucchini
6 tablespoons oil (olive oil is especially good with this)
Salt and fresh-ground pepper
2 cloves of garlic, finely chopped
½ teaspoon oregano
Chopped parsley

Wash zucchini, cut off stem ends and slice lengthwise into pencil-thin pieces about 3 inches long. Heat oil in a skillet and sauté zucchini over high heat until browned. Shake pan carefully to brown evenly. Add salt, pepper, garlic, and oregano. Cook about 5 minutes more over low heat. Transfer to warm serving dish and sprinkle with parsley.

CHAPTER 8

salads and salad dressings

DOs and DON'Ts for Making Salads

DO thoroughly wash and dry salad greens several hours before using and store in a towel in the refrigerator so that they will be dry, crisp, and cold when it's time to make the salad.

DO use a variety of salad greens such as Bibb, Boston, romaine, iceberg—whatever is in season. If possible, use two or three varieties.

DO add interest to your salad bowl by using herbs, grated hard-cooked eggs, slivers of ham and cheese, sliced green pepper, mushrooms, celery, anchovy, pimiento, capers, croutons, or anything else you happen to have on hand.

DO take good care of your wooden salad bowl, wiping it thoroughly dry after each use. Refrain from washing it if you possibly can.

DO make sure that everything, including the dressing, is ready ahead of time so that assembling the salad can be quickly accomplished.

DON'T make large quantities of salad dressing. Make it fresh the day you are using it.

DON'T toss salad in dressing a long time before the meal is served. If you do, your salad will be limp instead of crisp. Wait until the last minute.

DON'T include tomatoes when tossing a salad. Their juices will thin the salad dressing. Instead, marinate them in a small bowl in the same dressing that you are using for the salad. Then, using a slotted spoon, scatter them over the top of the tossed salad.

DON'T forget to keep fresh, chopped parsley on hand. Also, if possible, chopped chives.

TOSSED SALAD WITH EGG MAYONNAISE DRESSING
Salad greens

Egg Dressing
2 hard-cooked eggs
1 tablespoon finely chopped onion
1 tablespoon finely chopped parsley
Salt and fresh-ground pepper
2 tablespoons salad oil
1 tablespoon vinegar
¼ teaspoon Worcestershire sauce
4 tablespoons Mayonnaise
Fresh chopped parsley
Fresh chopped chives

Wash and dry salad greens and refrigerate. Chop eggs very fine with stainless steel knife. Put in a bowl with onion, parsley, salt, pepper, oil, vinegar, and Worcestershire sauce. Beat with a fork while adding the mayonnaise. Just before serving, put greens in salad bowl, pour over the dressing, toss lightly and sprinkle a little more parsley and chives over the bowl.

ASPARAGUS WITH CAPER DRESSING

Salad greens
24 fresh asparagus spears, cooked (when not in season, use
   canned or frozen)
⅓ cup red wine vinegar
1 tablespoon capers, drained and finely chopped
1 teaspoon salt
Fresh-ground pepper to taste
⅔ cup salad oil
1 teaspoon water
1 hard-cooked egg, grated
1 tablespoon chopped parsley

Store washed and dried salad greens and asparagus in the refrigerator. In a jar, combine vinegar, capers, salt, and pepper and shake hard. Add the oil and water and again shake very hard. Adjust seasoning to taste. Pour a little of the dressing over the asparagus. When ready to serve, arrange salad greens on platter (or individual plates) and arrange the asparagus on top. Spoon over some of the dressing and garnish with a sprinkling of grated egg and parsley.

STUFFED TOMATOES WITH MAYONNAISE

6 medium-sized tomatoes
Salt and fresh-ground pepper
Ground dill
½ pound marinated button mushrooms
Fresh chopped parsley

Skin tomatoes, cut off the tops, and scoop out most of the pulp. Turn upside down to drain a few minutes, then season inside and out with salt, pepper, and a pinch of dill. Place 3 or 4 marinated mushrooms inside each and store in the refrigerator to chill.

Mayonnaise Sour Cream Dressing

    1 pint Mayonnaise (preferably homemade)
    ½ pint sour cream
    1 teaspoon grated onion
    1 teaspoon lemon juice (fresh)
    ½–1 teaspoon curry powder

Blend all the ingredients and store, covered, in the refrigerator. Just before serving, spoon generously over each tomato and garnish with parsley.

NOTE: If you happen to have some lettuce, stand each tomato on a leaf just for decor. This is a hearty salad and requires no greens except for decoration.

Mushroom Marinade

    ½ pound fresh button mushrooms
    ⅔ cup vinegar
    ½ cup water
    1 bay leaf
    6 peppercorns
    2 teaspoons salt
    1 teaspoon sugar
    1 clove garlic, crushed
    2–3 whole cloves

Place all ingredients, except mushrooms, into a pint or larger jar. Seal jar and shake vigorously. Set aside. Prepare mushrooms by cutting off stems level with base. Rinse in cold water. Put mushrooms in jar of marinade. Seal, refrigerate for a few hours. Will keep for about a week.

VEGETABLE SALAD WITH SOUR CREAM DRESSING

    4 tomatoes
    1 small onion, finely chopped
    2 cups sliced cucumbers
    ½ cup sliced radishes
    1 cup coarsely chopped celery
    1½ cups shredded cabbage
    Salt and fresh-ground pepper

Sour Cream Dressing

1¼ cups sour cream
1 teaspoon seasoned salt
3 tablespoons vinegar
½ teaspoon sugar
1 teaspoon dry mustard
½ teaspoon paprika
A few drops of Worcestershire sauce

Skin the tomatoes, remove the pulp and seeds, and cut into small pieces. Combine tomatoes, onion, cucumbers, radishes, celery, and cabbage. Season with salt and pepper. Combine all the sour cream dressing ingredients. Lightly mix half of the dressing with the vegetables. When serving, spoon balance of dressing over the top.

COLE SLAW

1 medium-sized white cabbage (about 2 pounds)
1 medium-sized onion, grated
1 small carrot, grated
¼ green pepper, diced
Salt and fresh-ground pepper
½ teaspoon sugar
¼ teaspoon dry mustard
2 tablespoons salad oil
1 tablespoon vinegar (cider, wine, or herb)
5 tablespoons Mayonnaise
1 teaspoon lemon juice
1 teaspoon chopped parsley

Cut cabbage in four. Wash thoroughly. Cut away the hard stalk. Slice cabbage very thin, then chop coarsely. Put in a large bowl and grate in the onion and carrot. Add green pepper, salt, fresh-ground pepper, sugar, mustard, oil, and vinegar. Blend well. In a separate bowl mix together the mayonnaise and lemon juice and add to cabbage. Check the seasoning, arrange in a serving bowl, sprinkle with parsley, and keep in the refrigerator until ready to serve.

STUFFED AVOCADO

6 lettuce leaves
1 8-ounce package of cream cheese, at room temperature
1–2 teaspoons cream
6–8 pitted ripe olives, coarsely chopped
1 tablespoon chopped chives
1 teaspoon anchovy paste (or minced anchovies)
2 firm, large avocados
Juice of 1 lemon
3 cups salad greens
Tart French Dressing
Fresh chopped parsley

Prepare 6 large lettuce leaves and 3 cups chopped salad greens. Set aside. Soften the cream cheese with cream. Add olives, chives, and anchovy paste. Peel avocados carefully, cut in half, and remove stones. Fill cavity with cream cheese mixture. Press avocado halves together tightly and brush outside with lemon juice. Wrap each separately in wax paper and chill in refrigerator. When ready to serve, toss salad greens in French dressing. Make a bed of lettuce on each salad plate. Add salad greens. Cut avocados in thick, crosswise slices and put two slices on each salad. Sprinkle with parsley.

GERMAN-STYLE CUCUMBERS

3 long, thin cucumbers
Salt
6 tablespoons salad oil
4 tablespoons vinegar
Salt and fresh-ground pepper
Paprika
1 teaspoon fresh chopped chives
1 teaspoon fresh chopped parsley
Salad greens

Peel cucumbers and slice into rounds as thin as possible. Salt the slices well and place them in a bowl, pressed down by a heavy weight. Let stand in refrigerator for at least an hour. Drain, then squeeze cucumbers dry with hands. Make a French dressing with oil, vinegar, salt, pepper and a dash of paprika. Marinate cucumbers in this dressing. Add chives and parsley and serve on a bed of salad greens.

CUCUMBERS IN SOUR CREAM

3 long, thin cucumbers
Salt
1 cup sour cream
2 tablespoons lemon juice
1 teaspoon salt
Paprika, chives, fresh-ground pepper
Chopped parsley

Peel and slice cucumbers as thin as possible. Let stand for 1 hour in salted ice water. Drain and press dry with hands. Mix together sour cream, lemon juice, salt, paprika, chives, and pepper. Add to cucumbers, sprinkle with chopped parsley, and serve.

GREEN BEAN SALAD

1½ pounds fresh whole beans (or 2 packages frozen)
½ cup scallions, or onions, finely chopped
½ cup Tart French Dressing
Salt and fresh-ground pepper
½ cup sour cream
Chopped chives and dill
Chopped parsley

Cook beans and, whether fresh or frozen, "refresh" by pouring cold water over them immediately on removing from stove. In a bowl mix together the scallions and French dressing. Add beans, salt, and pepper. In another bowl blend sour cream, chives, and dill. Refrigerate covered. Just before serving, add the sour cream dressing to the beans and mix well. Sprinkle with parsley and serve.

SUNDAY NIGHT SALAD

Served with a loaf of garlic bread, dessert and coffee, this is a very popular meal.

2 heads iceberg lettuce, shredded
1½ cups chicken (or turkey) cut into julienne strips
1½ cups ham, cut into julienne strips
1 cup Swiss or Cheddar cheese in julienne strips, cut in two
2 large tomatoes, peeled and diced
2 tablespoons sweet pickle relish
Dressing
Fresh chopped parsley

Dressing

1 cup Mayonnaise
3 tablespoons cider vinegar
5 tablespoons salad oil
1 tablespoon chopped chives
4 hard-cooked eggs, coarsely chopped
1½ teaspoons salt
1 tablespoon Worcestershire sauce

To Make Dressing: Put mayonnaise in a bowl, beat in vinegar and oil alternately. When thoroughly blended, add remaining ingredients.

Place shredded lettuce in a large salad bowl. Arrange chicken, ham, cheese, tomatoes, and relish on lettuce. Pour dressing over salad and gently toss. Sprinkle parsley over top.

MUSHROOM SALAD

French Dressing ⚹1
1 pound fresh mushrooms, cut into bite-sized pieces
1 bunch celery, cut into bite-sized pieces
2 hard-cooked eggs, cut into chunks
2 tablespoons minced onion
2 pimientos, minced
Salt and fresh-ground pepper
Salad greens
Chopped parsley

Place mushrooms in a deep bowl. Add celery, including a few tiny top leaves. Add eggs, onion, and pimiento. Season with salt and pepper. Shake French dressing well and pour over mushrooms. Toss gently until well coated. In a salad bowl toss lightly salted salad greens in the same French dressing. Add mushroom mixture, and sprinkle with parsley.

CHICKEN SALAD DELUXE

  4 cups bite-sized pieces of cooked chicken
      (3 large breasts will be more than enough)
  1 cup coarsely chopped white stalks of celery
  Salt and fresh-ground pepper
  ¾–1 cup Mayonnaise
  2–3 tablespoons sour cream
  1 teaspoon grated onion
  1–2 teaspoons curry
  6 hard-cooked eggs
  3 tomatoes, peeled and quartered
  6 lettuce leaves
  3 cups salad greens
  Tart French Dressing
  3–4 tablespoons capers (optional)
  Chopped parsley

Combine chicken and celery in a bowl and season with salt and pepper. In a separate bowl blend together mayonnaise, sour cream, onion, and curry powder. Pour three quarters of this mixture over the chicken and toss lightly. Cover and refrigerate. Halve the eggs, season with salt and pepper and store with tomatoes in refrigerator on covered platter. Wash and dry lettuce leaves, wrap in cloth, and store with the rest of the salad ingredients. Have capers drained and parsley chopped.

   Just before serving, toss greens lightly in tart French dressing and arrange lettuce on platter. Add balance of mayonnaise dressing to chicken and mound in the center of the platter. Surround chicken with alternating egg halves and tomato wedges. Season again lightly with salt and pepper and sprinkle with capers and parsley.

TOMATO, ARTICHOKE, AND
CURRIED MAYONNAISE

2 large, ripe tomatoes (or 3 medium-sized)
6 canned artichoke hearts
Salad greens
Chopped chives
Chopped parsley

Dressing

1 cup Mayonnaise
½ cup sour cream
1 teaspoon fresh lemon juice
1 teaspoon grated onion
½–1 teaspoon curry powder
½ teaspoon dill weed (or 1 teaspoon fresh chopped dill)

Combine all ingredients for the dressing, blend well, pour into a bowl and refrigerate until ready to use. In another bowl pour boiling water on the tomatoes, let stand a few seconds, remove to cold water, then peel. Cut each into 3 equal, flat slices and season lightly with salt and pepper. Put artichoke hearts, sliced tomatoes, and washed and dried greens in refrigerator. Just before serving make a bed of lettuce on each plate. Spoon salad greens on the lettuce. Add one slice of tomato with an artichoke heart in the middle and spoon over a generous amount of dressing. Sprinkle with parsley and serve.

SPINACH, MUSHROOM, AND BACON SALAD

1 head Boston or Bibb lettuce
1 pound fresh, young spinach leaves
½ pound fresh mushrooms
½ cup Tart French Dressing
3 slices bacon, cooked until very crisp
Fresh chopped parsley
Salt and fresh-ground pepper

Wash and dry lettuce. Wash spinach in several changes of cold water. Remove the coarse stems. Dry spinach on paper towels and store in refrigerator with the lettuce. Wash and dry mushrooms and slice quite thin. Marinate in French dressing. When ready to serve, put salad greens and spinach in a salad bowl and season lightly and toss in the same French dressing. Spread the marinated mushrooms over the top with a slotted spoon and then crumble bacon over the mushrooms. Garnish with chopped parsley.

CAESAR SALAD

This may be prepared in advance and assembled at the last minute.

Croutons

    5 slices of white bread, crusts removed, and diced into
        ¼-inch cubes
    1 cup of oil

Heat the oil to 360 degrees and sauté bread cubes until golden. Remove croutons from hot oil with slotted spoon to paper towel.

    2 heads romaine lettuce, leaves separated, washed, and dried
    2 cloves garlic, minced
    1 small can anchovy fillets, finely chopped
    ½ teaspoon fresh-ground pepper
    2 whole eggs
    ½ cup olive oil
    6 tablespoons wine vinegar
    2 tablespoons chopped capers
    ½ cup grated cheese (Romano or Parmesan)
    Salt to taste

Break lettuce into bite-sized pieces in large salad bowl. Add minced garlic and anchovies, including the oil in which they were packed. Add fresh-ground pepper. Add 2 raw eggs and toss gently but thoroughly. Add olive oil, vinegar, and capers, then toss again. Add the croutons and cheese, toss lightly. Check for seasoning. Serve.

NOTE: We reserve salt to the last, as the anchovies may have provided adequate saltiness.

SALAD MOLLY

This salad is very hearty, very good, and easy to assemble. Espe-cially good served with toasted crackers and cottage cheese for a summer luncheon or Sunday night supper.

6 slices of ham
6 slices Swiss cheese
2 heads iceberg lettuce
1 cup Mayonnaise
½ cup chili sauce
Salt and fresh-ground pepper
Chopped parsley
Chopped chives

With a sharp knife slice ham and cheese into strips about 3 inches long. Shred lettuce. Wrap in a towel and refrigerate. Blend mayonnaise and chili sauce and store covered in refrigerator. When ready to assemble, put lettuce in salad bowl, add ham and cheese, and pour on dressing. Toss until thoroughly blended. Season lightly with salt and pepper and sprinkle with parsley and chives.

NOTE: Sliced boiled chicken or sliced turkey may be added.

TART FRENCH DRESSING

In a blender measure:

½ cup olive oil
½ cup salad oil
¼ cup cider vinegar
6 tablespoons red wine vinegar
1 tablespoon lemon juice
1 teaspoon prepared Dijon mustard
1 teaspoon salt
½ teaspoon sugar
½ teaspoon dill weed
½ teaspoon chives
1 large clove garlic (optional)

Whirl all ingredients *except clove of garlic* in blender until thoroughly mixed. Taste and adjust seasoning. Crush garlic clove and keep in the bottom of the jar containing the dressing. If dressing is too oily, mix in salt a bit at a time.

FRENCH DRESSING VARIATIONS

#1

¼ cup lemon juice
½ cup olive oil (or salad oil)
Salt and fresh-ground pepper
⅛ teaspoon garlic powder
¼ teaspoon sugar
½ teaspoon dill weed
½ teaspoon water

Put all ingredients in a jar and shake well. Correct seasoning.

#2

¼ cup vinegar (wine, cider, tarragon, or a mixture)
½ teaspoon salt
¼ teaspoon fresh-ground pepper
Pinch of dry mustard
¾ cup olive oil

Put vinegar in a bowl and add salt and pepper and the mustard. Stir mixture well. Beat dressing with a wire whisk or fork while slowly adding oil. Dressing will thicken. Correct seasoning.

#3

1 small clove garlic, minced
½ teaspoon dry mustard
½ teaspoon salt
½ teaspoon fresh-ground pepper
1 teaspoon finely chopped onion (or scallions or chives)
½ teaspoon sugar
½ cup plus 2 tablespoons olive or corn oil
5 tablespoons white wine vinegar (or half vinegar and half
    lemon juice)

Put all ingredients in a screw-top jar and shake hard. Correct the seasoning. Most dressings need additional salt.

NOTE: By elimination of garlic or garlic powder, French dressing can be used over fruits.

SALADS AND SALAD DRESSINGS   131

ROQUEFORT DRESSING

#1

¼ cup vinegar
½ teaspoon salt
A few shakes of fresh-ground pepper
½ cup olive (or salad) oil
2 tablespoons heavy cream
¼ cup crumbled Roquefort cheese
1 teaspoon lemon juice

Put vinegar in a bowl with salt and pepper and mix with wire whisk.

NOTE: Bleu cheese may be used in place of Roquefort.

#2

2 tablespoons Mayonnaise
2 tablespoons crumbled Roquefort cheese (or Bleu cheese)
½ cup Tart French Dressing
½ teaspoon Worcestershire sauce
Salt to taste

Thoroughly mix mayonnaise and cheese. Slowly add French dressing, blending well with wire whisk. Add Worcestershire sauce and salt.

VINAIGRETTE DRESSING

¾ cup olive (or salad) oil
¼ cup vinegar (wine, tarragon, or cider)
Salt and fresh-ground pepper
½ teaspoon dry mustard
2 shallots or scallions, finely chopped
2 hard-cooked eggs, finely chopped
1 small pickle, chopped fine
1 teaspoon finely chopped pimiento
1 teaspoon chopped capers

Combine oil, vinegar, salt, pepper, and mustard in a jar. Cover and shake well. Add shallots, eggs, pickle, and pimiento and capers and stir until well blended.

BLENDER MAYONNAISE

1 cup salad oil
1 egg
2 tablespoons lemon juice
¼ teaspoon dry mustard
½ teaspoon salt
Dash of cayenne pepper

Put one quarter of the oil in the blender. Add remaining ingredients and blend at medium speed for 15 seconds. Remove top and very slowly, at first, start adding the rest of the oil. As soon as it begins to show signs of blending and thickening, add remainder in a steady stream. Adding the oil should take about 20 seconds. Taste, and adjust seasoning if necessary.

All salad dressings need a little adjusting as we have stressed. If you do not make your own mayonnaise (very good it is!) buy the best commercial brand you can find and add 1 teaspoon of fresh lemon juice to each half cup. It makes a great difference.

desserts

For some reason people tend to remember the dessert served at any given party long after all else has been forgotten. Perhaps desserts are so important because we carry over a "sweet tooth" from childhood, linked to good behavior and rewards. No matter the reason, desserts are popular and important. They can range from simple fruit, accompanied by delectable cookies, to rich concoctions. At buffet supper parties we have often seen a platter of two or three different kinds of cookies create a sensation by themselves. Desserts should relate to what has been served before—a hearty dinner requires a light dessert and vice versa. Here are some of each.

LEMON CHEESE PIE

Pie Crust

1½ cups graham cracker crumbs
¾ stick butter, melted
¼ cup sugar
¼ teaspoon cinnamon

Mix together crust ingredients and line a 9-inch pie plate with the crumbs, reserving about ¼ cup to garnish the topping. Press the crumbs gently and evenly with the back of your fingers or press an 8″ pie plate over crumbs. Bake in a 375-degree oven for 8–10 minutes. Cool.

Filling

1½ large packages of cream cheese at room
    temperature, (12 ounces)
2 eggs
½ cup sugar
1–2 tablespoons fresh lemon juice
    or
1–2 tablespoons rum

Beat together all ingredients until smooth and free from lumps. Pour into pie crust and spread evenly. Bake in a 375-degree oven for 20 minutes (or a little longer if center appears slightly soft).

Topping

1 cup sour cream
4 tablespoons sugar
1 tablespoon fresh lemon juice
    or
1 tablespoon rum

While pie is baking, mix together topping ingredients and blend well. When baked, remove pie from oven and spread with topping. Sprinkle reserved crumbs over the top and return to oven (same temperature) for 5 minutes. Cool, and serve at room temperature.

NOTE: If made ahead, store in refrigerator with wax paper on the shelf above for protection. Remove from refrigerator about an hour before serving.

DESSERTS   135

BOMBE FAVORITE WITH MELBA SAUCE

Requested from us and printed in Gourmet *magazine*

10 half shells of meringue
1 pint heavy cream
2 tablespoons confectioners' sugar
1 teaspoon vanilla
2 ounces kirsch or white rum

Meringue Shells

4 egg whites
8 ounces superfine granulated sugar
Cookie tins covered with brown paper (can use grocery bags, cut
    up)
Pastry bag and plain tube (if available—not necessary)

To Make Meringue Shells: Beat the egg whites until almost stiff, add 2 tablespoons of sugar, and continue beating a few seconds more. Then fold in balance of sugar and beat until very stiff. Pipe (or spoon) into 3–4-inch heaping rounds on the brown paper. Bake in a 250-degree oven for about 45 minutes. Should feel crisp to the touch—if not, bake a little longer. Remove from oven, remove meringue shells from paper, and transfer to a platter to cool.

Whip the cream, fold in sugar, vanilla, and kirsch. Lightly oil a 10-inch spring-form. Break the meringue shells into large pieces and mix gently with the whipped cream mixture. Spoon into spring-form, press down lightly, cover with a round of wax paper and store in freezer for at least 6 hours before serving. (Will keep for weeks.)

Melba Sauce

1 pint fresh or frozen raspberries
6–8 ounces confectioners' sugar, sifted
1 ounce kirsch or white rum

With a wooden spoon, rub fresh or defrosted raspberries through a metal sieve into a bowl. Gradually stir in confectioners' sugar. When the mixture is the consistency of thin cream enough sugar has been added. Then add kirsch or rum.

When ready to serve, remove bombe from spring-form to a cold platter, cut into portions, and spoon on a little Melba sauce. Serve balance of sauce in a sauce boat.

CHOCOLATE ALMOND TORTE

1 8-inch round cake pan, lightly buttered and floured
4 ounces semi-sweet chocolate
2 tablespoons strong liquid coffee
1 stick butter (softened)
⅔ cup sugar
3 eggs, separated
½ cup ground almonds
¾ cup sifted flour
2 drops almond extract

Melt chocolate in double boiler with coffee. Cream butter in bowl, then add sugar by degrees and cream them together. Beat egg whites until stiff, but not dry. Add butter to coffee-chocolate mixture. Add the yolks, ground almonds, sifted flour, and almond extract. Mix well. Batter should be rather stiff. Fold in beaten egg whites. Turn into baking pan, and bake for 20–25 minutes at 350 degrees. Cake should be done on the edges but slightly moist in center. Remove cake from oven and cool a little. Run thin-bladed knife around edge of pan. Place large dinner plate over cake. Flip over, and cake will turn out onto plate.

Frosting

3 ounces semi-sweet chocolate
1 teaspoon liquid coffee
2 tablespoons butter
1 tablespoon brandy
Toasted almond halves for garnish

Melt the chocolate in double boiler with the liquid coffee. Add butter and brandy. Stir well. (Chocolate should now be a flowing liquid. If too thick add 2 tablespoons hot water and blend well.) Pour warm frosting over cake and spread with spatula, allowing frosting to run a little over the sides. Garnish with toasted almond halves.

COCOANUT TORTE

2 cups shredded cocoanut
4 eggs, separated
1 cup sugar
1 cup Zwiebach crumbs
1 teaspoon baking powder
⅛ teaspoon salt
1 teaspoon vanilla
½ pint heavy cream

Preheat oven to 350 degrees. Place cocoanut on a baking sheet and toast in oven until a golden color (about 10 minutes, but watch it). Beat egg yolks, then add sugar and beat until thick and lemon-colored.

In a bowl mix the Zwiebach crumbs, baking powder, salt, and 1½ cups of cocoanut. Fold in the vanilla and stiffly beaten egg whites. Pour into 2 greased and floured 8-inch cake pans and bake in a 375-degree oven for about 35–40 minutes (or until a golden layers and over cake. Sprinkle remaining cocoanut over the top. brown). Cool, then turn out. Spread whipped cream between

ORANGE CAKE GRAND MARNIER

3 cups sifted cake flour
4 teaspoons baking powder
½ teaspoon salt
1½ sticks butter, at room temperature
1¾ cups sugar
3 eggs, well beaten
½ cup orange juice
1 tablespoon lemon juice
½ cup water
Grated rind of 1 orange

Sift together flour, baking powder, and salt. Cream butter, then beat in sugar. Add eggs and blend well. Add flour mixture and stir until absorbed. In another bowl mix together orange juice, lemon juice, water, and rind. In a large bowl beat together one third of the batter and one third of the liquid. Blend well, then add second third of each, and finally the last third. Pour into three oiled (or buttered) 8-inch cake tins and bake in a 350-degree oven for 30 minutes. Remove from tins and cool.

Filling

¾ pint heavy cream
4 tablespoons confectioners' sugar
2 tablespoons Grand Marnier
2–3 mandarin oranges, or 1 11-ounce can segments
Grated rind of 1 orange

Whip cream, add sugar, and blend well. Add Grand Marnier. Place one cake layer on large platter, spread with whipped cream mixture, and cover with second layer. Spread again with whipped cream and cover with third layer, frosting top and sides. Drain orange segments and arrange around top of cake. Sprinkle with orange rind. Refrigerate until ready to serve.

MYSTERY ICE CREAM MOLD

This one is for the time when you'd like to serve a delicious home-made dessert and haven't time to make it. It is immensely popular and can be made in 5 minutes.

1 box peanut brittle (10-ounce)
1½ quarts vanilla or coffee ice cream

Break peanut brittle into pieces and chop in blender until crumbs. Reserve ¼–½ cup. Put ice cream into a large bowl and let stand 4–5 minutes (or until it is just soft enough to stir in the peanut brittle crumbs). Quickly blend the two and spoon into a spring-form, an ice cream mold—whatever you happen to have. Sprinkle the reserved crumbs on top, cover with aluminum foil, and store in freezer. When ready to serve, slide a knife gently around the spring-form rim. Remove rim, transfer ice cream to platter and serve at once. If you happen to have a little butterscotch sauce to dribble over the top, it does no harm.

You can make this same dessert using cut up leftover Party Brownies and decorate top with slivered semi-sweet chocolate.

SOUR CREAM COFFEE CAKE

This one is excellent for breakfast, lunch, or dinner

1 stick butter, at room temperature
1 cup sugar
2 eggs
1 teaspoon vanilla
2 cups sifted flour
1½ teaspoons baking powder
½ teaspoon baking soda
1 cup sour cream

Filling

½ cup brown sugar (light or dark)   ⎫
½ cup chopped nuts   ⎬ mixed together
1 teaspoon cinnamon   ⎬ in a small bowl
2 teaspoons flour   ⎭
1 regulation-sized bread pan or 2 small ones. Butter pans lightly,
    line with aluminum foil, and butter foil

To Make the Cake: Cream butter, add sugar and cream together. Mix in eggs and vanilla. Sift together flour, baking powder, and soda. Add flour mixture and sour cream *alternately* to butter-sugar mixture blending until all are used. Pour half the mixture into the loaf pan and cover with three fourths of the filling. *Reserve balance of filling for the top.* Cover the filling with balance of batter and sprinkle remaining filling over the entire top. Bake for 1 hour in a preheated 350-degree oven. Cool, run a sharp knife around the rim and gently lift out of pan (or pans).

DATE AND NUT TORTE

4 eggs
1 cup sugar
1 cup cake flour
2 teaspoons baking powder
¼ teaspoon salt
1 cup coarsely chopped walnut meats (or pecans)
1 cup dates, cut up
½ teaspoon vanilla
½ pint heavy cream, whipped

Preheat oven to 325 degrees. Beat eggs lightly, then add sugar gradually. Sift together ¾ cup flour, the baking powder, and the salt and add to egg mixture. In a separate bowl mix together dates, nuts, and remaining ¼ cup of flour. Fold into the egg mixture. Bake in spring-form, or cake pan, for 45–50 minutes. Cool and serve with side dish of whipped cream.

WALNUT MERINGUE TORTE

Prepare two 8-inch round cake pans by buttering the bottom and sides of pans and dusting lightly with flour. Cut 2 rounds of wax or parchment paper and put one on the bottom of each pan. Butter the paper lightly and dust with flour.

    4 egg whites
    1 cup plus 2 tablespoons sugar
    ¼ teaspoon vanilla
    ½ teaspoon vinegar
    ¾ cup ground (or finely chopped) walnuts
    ½ cup heavy cream
    1 cup fresh raspberries, or 1½ cups fresh strawberries
    Confectioners' sugar

Beat egg whites until almost stiff, then, slowly, while beating, add half of the sugar. Beat in the vanilla and vinegar, then the rest of the sugar. Fold in the nuts. Pour mixture into prepared pans. Bake in a preheated 350-degree oven for 30–40 minutes. Meringues should be firm and slightly browned. Remove from oven, cool a few minutes, then run a sharp knife around the rim. To remove cakes from pan, cover each with a large plate, face side down, and flip over quickly. Meringues will drop onto plate. Peel off the paper. While meringues are cooling, whip cream with 1–2 table-spoons confectioners' sugar. Spread cream on one meringue and set raspberries (or strawberries) into the cream. Cover with second meringue. Sprinkle top with confectioners' sugar.

VARIATION—increase quantity of whipped cream and berries and fill middle layer with cream and sliced berries and top meringue with cream and whole berries.

GALETTE NORMANDE

Pastry

> 2½ cups flour
> 2 sticks butter
> 1 cup confectioners' sugar
> 3 egg yolks
> 1 teaspoon vanilla extract

Sift flour on a board. Make a well in the center and place butter, confectioners' sugar, egg yolks, and vanilla in the well. With tips of fingers, draw in the flour and work to a smooth paste. Make into a ball, roll in wax paper and place in refrigerator for about an hour. Meanwhile, prepare filling.

Filling

> 3 pounds cooking apples
> 1 tablespoon butter
> 1 lemon (grated rind and juice)
> 3–4 tablespoons sugar (more if apples are tart)

Wash the apples. Cut into quarters and core. Melt butter in a saucepan, add the apples and the grated lemon rind and juice. Cover and cook over low heat until soft and pulpy. Rub apples through a strainer. Return apple purée to saucepan. Add the sugar, and cook over medium heat, stirring, until purée becomes thick and clear. Set aside.

Divide pastry into 3 equal pieces. Roll out or pat into rounds (about 8 inches in diameter) of equal size. (You may find it more convenient to roll or pat out these rounds on the back of a cookie tin.) Bake on back of cookie tin in a preheated 375-degree oven until a *pale* golden color (12–15 minutes). Cool pastry. Remove 1 pastry round gently to a large flat dish. Spoon on half the apple marmalade purée. Place second pastry round on top and repeat. Place third round on top and set aside.

Topping

> ½ pint heavy cream
> 3 tablespoons confectioners' sugar
> 2 tablespoons brandy
> Walnut halves for decoration

In a cold bowl whip the cream. Add the confectioners' sugar and the brandy. Decorate top of cake with a smooth layer of brandied whipped cream. Place walnut halves in any pattern. (You may also use fresh strawberries or glazed fruits.)

CHOCOLATE MOUSSE PIE

Pie Crust

> 1¼ cups graham cracker crumbs (or gingersnap crumbs) finely rolled or ground in the blender
> ½ cup sugar
> ½ stick butter, melted

Mix ingredients together and press evenly onto bottom and sides of a 9-inch pie pan. Bake in a 375-degree oven for 8 minutes. Remove from oven and cool.

Filling

> 10 ounces semi-sweet chocolate
> ½ cup strong coffee (liquid)
> 2 tablespoons butter
> 4 eggs, separated
> 2 tablespoons rum, brandy, or kirsch

Place chocolate and coffee in top of double boiler and cook over medium heat until chocolate has melted and the mixture thickened a little. Remove from heat and beat in the butter, then the egg yolks, *one at a time*. In a separate bowl, beat egg whites until they hold a stiff peak. Fold whites into chocolate mixture gently with a metal spoon. Fold in rum and pour mixture into pie crust and refrigerate for at least 3 hours before serving.

Garnish

> 1 cup heavy cream
> 2 tablespoons sugar
> 1 ounce semi-sweet chocolate

Whip cream, add the sugar, and spread cream over the pie. Scrape semi-sweet chocolate with a vegetable parer over the entire top and refrigerate until ready to serve.

PARTY BROWNIES

1. *Melt together*
    4 squares unsweetened chocolate
    2 sticks butter

2. *Beat*
    4 eggs and then beat in
    2 cups sugar

3. *Combine*
    1 cup flour, unsifted
    ½ teaspoon salt
    1 cup chopped nuts
    1 teaspoon vanilla

Combine ⚹1, ⚹2, and ⚹3. Mix well together. Pour into a buttered 13×9×1½-inch pan. Bake 30–35 minutes in a preheated 325-degree oven.

Frosting
    2 tablespoons butter, softened at room temperature
    1¼ cups confectioners' sugar (sifted)
    3 tablespoons light cream

Beat butter; add sugar and beat. Add cream and mix until smooth. Spread mixture evenly over brownies.

Icing
    2 squares (2 ounces) semi-sweet chocolate
    1 tablespoon butter

Melt together chocolate and butter in small pan. With a wire whisk or fork, dribble over the top of the frosting in quick circles, or up and down and across.

NOTE: If you have any of these delectable brownies left, break them into small pieces and mix with coffee ice cream (see Mystery Ice Cream Mold).

THE BEACH PLUM INN COOKBOOK

PINEAPPLE RUM UPSIDE DOWN CAKE

To be made in a 9×1½-inch cake pan.

To prepare base

1 cup sugar
1 cup water
Juice of ½ lemon
1 fresh pineapple, carefully peeled, cut into ½-inch slices and
    center core removed

Place sugar and water in saucepan. Add lemon juice and stir gently until sugar is dissolved. Place pineapple slices in the sugar syrup and cook gently over medium heat for about 30 minutes. Allow to cool in the syrup.

To finish base

½ cup butter
1 cup light brown sugar
Maraschino cherries or pecan halves

Melt butter in the cake pan. Spread brown sugar evenly over the butter and arrange the pineapple slices on the brown sugar. Halve a few cherries (or use pecans) and set halves *cut side up* in the holes and around the pineapple. Create your own design.

Cake Filling

1 cup cake flour
1 teaspoon baking powder } sifted together
⅛ teaspoon salt
3 eggs, separated
1 cup sugar
3 tablespoons syrup from the pineapple
2 tablespoons rum

Place sifted flour, baking powder, and salt in a mixing bowl. In another bowl beat egg yolks until light, adding sugar gradually. Add pineapple syrup, rum, and sifted flour. Fold in the stiffly beaten egg whites and pour this batter over the pineapple arrangement. Bake in a 375-degree oven for 30–35 minutes, or until cake begins to leave the edges of the pan. While hot, cover cake with a serving plate and quickly turn upside down. Serve cake at room temperature. If desired, serve with a bowl of rum-flavored whipped cream.

PAVLOVA

Lightly butter a 9-inch or 10-inch pie plate (Pyrex is best) and pre-heat oven to 250 degrees.

¾ cup egg whites (6 or 7, depending on size)
⅛ teaspoon salt
1½ cups sugar
Whatever fresh fruit is available—raspberries, berries, sliced
    peaches, slightly sweetened with confectioners' sugar and a
    few drops of fresh lemon juice
½ pint heavy cream

Place the egg whites in a large bowl, add salt, and beat until stiff but still shiny. Beat in 1 tablespoon sugar, then gradually the balance of the sugar. When mixture is thick and satiny, fill the bottom of the pie plate to a thickness of about 1 inch, then spoon or pipe the balance around the edge, making a nest with a rim 2–3 inches high. Put in preheated oven and bake for about 1 hour (or a little longer—until it feels crisp and firm to the touch). Remove from oven and cool. When ready to serve; fill the center with fruit and either mask with whipped cream (which can be made earlier, covered, and stored in the refrigerator) or serve the whipped cream in a separate bowl (as a concession to calorie-conscious guests). Serve this dessert in the dish in which it was baked.

NOTE: Any recipe calling for egg whites only is best made on a dry, sunny day, which insures crispness. The yolks can be used for Hollandaise sauce, grated garnish on green vegetables (asparagus, spinach, broccoli, etc.), egg sandwiches, mayonnaise, garnish for the salad bowl, and other ways that you will invent.

CHOCOLATE ROULADE

5 eggs, separated
¾ cup sugar
6 ounces semi-sweet chocolate, coarsely chopped
1¼ cups heavy cream
¼ teaspoon vanilla
3 tablespoons confectioners' sugar

Line a cookie tin with parchment or bakers' paper, lightly greased and floured (tap off excess flour). Set oven at 375 degrees.

Beat egg yolks until thick and lemon-colored, then add the sugar and beat together until well blended. Put aside. Slowly melt the chocolate in the top of a double boiler. Cool, then stir into the egg-sugar mixture.

Beat the egg whites until stiff, then gently fold into the yolk mixture. Spread on paper-lined cookie tin. Bake for 17–20 minutes (or until just firm). Remove from oven and cool. Lightly cover with plastic wrap or wax paper and let stand a few hours.

To finish: Dust a second sheet of parchment (or bakers' paper) with confectioners' sugar. Remove covering from cake and flip quickly upside down on the sugar-dusted paper. Gently peel back the baking paper on which the cake was baked. Whip the cream until thick, flavor with the vanilla and confectioners' sugar, and spread over the cake. Holding ends of paper, gently roll cake onto a serving tray or platter. Cake may now be served as is, or lightly dusted with confectioners' sugar or decorated with grated chocolate, or whipped cream.

COCOANUT ALMOND MACAROONS

For best results line cookie tin with parchment paper, ungreased, which can be purchased at a stationery store in large sheets. The macaroons lift off more easily with this than brown paper or foil.

¾ cup sugar
½ cup confectioners' sugar
3 tablespoons cake flour
¼ teaspoon salt
4 egg whites
⅔ cup slivered almonds
½ teaspoon vanilla (or almond extract)
2 cups shredded cocoanut

Garnish

Maraschino cherries, or almonds cut in two, or glazed fruit bits

In a large bowl sift together both sugars, flour, and salt. Beat egg whites until they stand in firm peaks, then add 3 tablespoons of the sugar-flour mixture. Blend well and keep on beating, then add one quarter of remaining sugar-flour mixture and repeat until everything is blended and stiff. Fold in the slivered almonds, vanilla, and cocoanut. Let stand for about ten minutes, then drop by tablespoons onto cookie tin. Garnish with whatever you choose from above list and bake 20–25 minutes at 325 degrees or until a golden color. Let cool for a few minutes, then remove from paper and store in a cookie tin with a tight lid. They will keep for about one week.

DATE NUT SUGAR COOKIES

1 stick of butter
1 cup sugar
1 egg, beaten
¼ cup milk
¼ teaspoon vanilla
2 cups flour
2 teaspoons baking powder

Filling

½ stick butter, melted
½ cup chopped dates
1 tablespoon cinnamon
½ cup chopped walnuts
½ cup sugar

Cream the butter and sugar. Add the egg, milk, and vanilla. Mix together the baking powder and 1 cup of the flour and combine mixtures. When well blended, add the second cup of flour. Form into a ball and chill in refrigerator.

When ready to bake, roll out on a floured board and lightly brush melted butter over dough. Sprinkle with dates, cinnamon, walnuts, and sugar. Roll up like a jelly roll and cut into 1-inch slices. Bake on a greased cookie sheet in a 375-degree oven for 20–25 minutes.

PEGGY'S GLAZED COOKIES

These are unlike most cookies. They are very thin, very crisp, uniquely delicious, and if carefully packed in a cookie tin with waxed paper between each layer will keep perfectly for at least three weeks. Take your time making them—this recipe will produce 60–70—and the end results are beautiful.

2 sticks of butter, at room temperature
1 cup sugar
1 egg
1 teaspoon vanilla
2 cups all-purpose flour, sifted with
a pinch of salt
½ cup slivered or sliced almonds
Teflon cookie tins
Large cooling rack

Cream butter and sugar. Add egg and vanilla and when well blended gradually stir in the flour. Put some extra flour in a bowl to dip hands in occasionally to keep batter from sticking. Roll dough into small balls placed about 1½ inches apart on the cookie tin.

When the cookie tin is filled with balls, take a glass with a diameter of about 2½ inches, plus two small dishes—one containing water and the other about ½ cup of granulated sugar. Dip the glass lightly into the water, then into the sugar, and then gently press down a cookie ball. Repeat until all are flat and lightly coated with water and sugar. Sprinkle a few slivered almonds on each, or arrange a pattern—whatever you choose—and put in a preheated 350-degree oven for about 8–10 minutes. Check—cookies should be off-white and have a lovely glaze.

Remove from oven and gently loosen in the pan immediately. Let stand for about 2 minutes, then carefully remove to large cake rack. When they are cool and crisp, pack them in cookie jars or tins, making sure they are airtight. The only real problem is that they disappear too quickly and everyone asks for the recipe.

FRUIT BRULÉE

This can be made during the summer with fresh fruit but any time with canned.

1 30-ounce can freestone peaches (halved or sliced)
1 14-ounce can apricot halves, pitted
1 14-ounce can pineapple chunks
1 14-ounce can purple plums
Grated rind of 1 orange
Grated rind of 1 lemon
Juice of ½ orange
Juice of ½ lemon
½ cup dark brown sugar
¼ cup gingersnap crumbs
1½ cups light brown sugar
½ pint sour cream

Drain fruit well (save fruit juices for many uses). Arrange attractively in layers in a buttered casserole. Mix together orange and lemon rind, then orange and lemon juice. Pour juices over fruit and then the rinds. Mix together dark brown sugar and gingersnap crumbs and sprinkle over fruit. Bake in a preheated 350-degree oven for about 20 minutes, basting once or twice. Reduce heat to 300 degrees and bake until syrup is fairly thick (about 30 minutes), again basting once or twice. Cool. At your convenience sift light brown sugar over entire surface of fruit in a ⅛–¼-inch layer. Turn on broiler and when *very* hot, put fruit about 6 inches beneath the heat. Watch carefully!! Within a minute or two the brown sugar will begin to melt. When it is all melted remove at once from oven. The whole process takes only about 3 minutes. Let dish stand at room temperature (it will now have a crust on top). If you prefer, store in the refrigerator and serve cold. Good hot, cold, or medium, served with sour cream in a sauce boat.

PINEAPPLE WITH KIRSCH SAUCE

1 large ripe pineapple
¼–½ cup sugar
Kirsch to taste (2–3 tablespoons)

Peel and core pineapple and cut into large dice. Sprinkle with sugar and kirsch and chill in refrigerator for at least 3 hours.

Sauce

  3 egg yolks
  3 tablespoons sugar
  ½ stick butter
  3 tablespoons liquid drained from pineapple

In the top of a double boiler, over medium heat, beat together the egg yolks and sugar. When well blended, add the butter, cut into small pieces and cook together, beating steadily, until it has thickened. Add 3 tablespoons liquid drained from refrigerated pineapple. Let sauce cool. When ready to serve, place the chilled pineapple in a glass or crystal bowl and spoon over sauce.

STRAWBERRIES ESCOFFIER

  1½ quarts strawberries, cleaned and hulled
  2 oranges, washed and dried
  ½ cup lump sugar
  ⅓ cup brandy or Grand Marnier
  1 pint heavy cream
  5 tablespoons confectioners' sugar
  ½ teaspoon vanilla

Place strawberries in a deep bowl. Holding orange firmly, rub sugar lumps over it one at a time. The sugar will absorb the orange zest, and in doing so will become orange-colored. Remove as much zest juice as you can with the lump sugar. Place the sugar in a small bowl. Squeeze the juice from the oranges onto the sugar. Crush the sugar in the juice. Add the brandy to the juice and dissolve the sugar. Pour this liquid over the strawberries and refrigerate for at least an hour. Whip the cream with confectioners' sugar and vanilla. Serve strawberries in a glass bowl at room temperature with whipped cream in a sauce dish.

POIRES EN SURPRISE

This one is so good that it's worth a little extra effort.

Sugar Syrup

    1 pound granulated sugar
    1 pint cold water
    1 teaspoon vanilla
    1 cup hot water
    Pastry brush
    6 medium-sized ripe pears

Combine sugar, water, and vanilla in pan over medium heat and stir along bottom of pan to prevent the sugar from settling while mixture comes to a boil. As it nears the boiling point, sugar crystals may form along the sides of the pan. Brush them down with the pastry brush, dipped in a glass of hot water. When sugar syrup comes to a boil, remove pan from heat and set aside. Peel pears, cut them in half lengthwise, and core them. Gently place them in sugar syrup and poach them, uncovered, over medium heat for about 1 hour. Remove from stove and let pears cool in the syrup.

Toasted Almonds

    ½ cup slivered almonds
    1 egg white, beaten until foamy
    2 tablespoons sugar

Toss almonds in beaten egg white. Remove, drain slightly, and sprinkle with sugar. Put on cookie pans and toast in a 325-degree oven. Keep an eye on them as they color rapidly. Remove when golden.

Sauce Suchard

    8 ounces semi-sweet chocolate
    1 cup syrup (use syrup in which pears were poached)
    2 tablespoons rum
    2 egg yolks
    ¼ cup light cream

Break chocolate into small pieces and melt in top of double boiler over simmering water. Stir until smooth, then add the syrup and rum. Keep warm but not hot. Beat the egg yolks with the cream and stir into the chocolate mixture. Keep warm, but do not boil. (If made ahead, sauce can be refrigerated and reheated in double boiler when ready to use.)

1½ quarts French vanilla ice cream

When ready to assemble this dessert, place a scoop of ice cream in 6 individual glass or china bowls. Place 2 pear halves over the ice cream, cavity side down. Sprinkle toasted almonds over the top. Serve warmed sauce Suchard separately in sauce boat and allow guests to help themselves.

miscellaneous musts

This chapter contains recipes that do not fall into any of the preceding categories but which we feel should be included.

CHEESE ROLLS

1 loaf unsliced day-old bread
⅓ cup grated Cheddar cheese
¼ cup spicy or French mustard
¼ cup melted butter

With sharp knife cut end crust from bread. Mix together cheese and mustard. Spread mixture over end of loaf. Cut thin slice from this end, trim off crust, and set aside. Repeat until you have 12 thin, crustless, slices of bread, spread with the mustard-cheese mixture. Brush melted butter on top of mustard mixture and roll each slice and cut in half. Place on cookie tin, seam side down, close together. Bake in a 350-degree oven until crisp and lightly browned. Serve with soups, salads, or cocktails.

CREPES

Crepes are versatile—they can be turned into Crepes Pralines, Crepes Suzette, Crepes aux Cerises, and dozens of other desserts. They can also be turned into delicious entrees—seafood crepes, chicken and mushroom, spinach and ham, etc. With a few dozen crepes in the freezer, you are ready for unexpected company at any time. Cookbooks are full of good suggestions for either kind, but here is our best recipe for the crepe itself.

¾ cup flour
Pinch of salt
1 whole egg
1 egg yolk
1¼ cups milk
1½ tablespoons melted butter

Sift flour and salt into a large bowl. Make a well in the center and deposit egg and yolk. Slowly add half of the milk while working flour very gradually into the eggs. While some of the flour is still unworked, add the melted butter, then, slowly, the rest of the milk and flour. If still lumpy, beat a little with egg beater. Let stand in refrigerator for at least an hour (can be overnight).

To Make Crepes: Heat a small omelet pan with a little oil. When hot, pour a small amount of batter into pan. Tip and roll until bottom of pan is thinly covered. When browned underneath (lift up one edge to inspect—usually about 1 minute) turn with a spatula and brown other side. Turn out on a cake rack (first side down) and repeat. If using that same day, cover with a dish towel after each addition. If freezing, separate each crepe with a square of wax paper and divide into numbered packages.

NOTE: Once you have the knack you can use two pans at a time.

CHEESE SOUFFLÉ (for 4)

4 tablespoons butter
4 tablespoons flour
1 cup milk
2 cups grated sharp Cheddar cheese
Salt
Dash of black and cayenne pepper
1 tablespoon Worcestershire sauce
½ teaspoon dry mustard
4 egg yolks
5 egg whites
425-degree oven

1. Tie a collar of aluminum foil around a 2-quart soufflé dish so that it stands about 2 inches above the rim. Butter soufflé dish and aluminum foil.

2. In a saucepan melt butter, remove from stove and stir in *sifted flour*. During this time bring milk to a boil. Return butter-flour mixture to medium heat and, when bubbling, add milk all at once, stirring steadily with a wire whisk. Continue stirring until mixture is thick and smooth. Remove from stove.

3. While hot, add cheese, stirring until melted. Season to taste with salt, peppers, Worcestershire sauce, and mustard. Cool slightly, then add *well-beaten egg yolks*.

NOTE: This much can be done hours ahead. Run cold water over a piece of wax paper, shake well, and cover soufflé with the damp wax paper touching mixture. This will prevent a crust from forming and you can finish it at your convenience. Store in the refrigerator.

4. Have soufflé at room temperature half an hour before baking. Beat egg whites with a pinch of salt until stiff. With a metal spoon quickly and gently fold into soufflé mixture, then turn into prepared soufflé dish. Bake in a 425-degree oven for 30–35 minutes (until a firm, golden brown). It can bake another 10 minutes (at 350 degrees) if you are delayed, but don't open oven door! Serve immediately on removing from oven, using two tablespoons. Chutney is a fine accompaniment.

VARIATIONS—Once you've made this, you may want to experiment further. For example—in addition to the cheese, add 1½ cups of finely chopped lobster or chicken. Or 1 cup flaked tuna or flounder which has been seasoned with 1–2 teaspoons of fresh lemon juice. Or diced ham with sautéed mushrooms, or finely chopped spinach.

CASSEROLE CHEESE SOUFFLÉ

Can be made the day before!!!

Filling

½ stick butter
1 large onion, finely chopped
1 pound mushrooms, finely chopped
1 tablespoon flour
3–4 tablespoons heavy cream
Salt and fresh-ground pepper

Melt butter and sauté onion until transparent. Add mushrooms, sauté until juices begin to run, then add flour, cream, salt, and pepper. Mix thoroughly and reserve.

Soufflé

4 cups milk
1 cup *unsifted* flour
8 eggs
6 tablespoons butter, at room temperature
Salt and fresh-ground pepper
Shake of cayenne pepper
1 teaspoon Worcestershire sauce
2 cups grated Swiss cheese
½ cup Parmesan cheese, or Romano (optional)

Scald milk, add flour, blend well, and cook for 3–4 minutes, stirring constantly, until quite thick. Remove from heat, cool a bit, and beat in, *one at a time,* the 8 eggs. Add butter, seasoning, and cheese. In a lightly buttered rectangular ovenproof glass dish, pour about half the soufflé. Spoon the onion-mushroom mixture over the top, then cover with balance of soufflé. Dust top with a light sprinkling of Parmesan and a little paprika. If baking at once, put into pre-heated 400-degree oven for *30 minutes.* If making ahead (which you can do the day before) remove from refrigerator and put into the preheated 400-degree oven for *45 minutes.*

CINNAMON BREAD

If you've never made bread before but own a mixer with a dough-hook attachment, you will have no trouble making this most delicious bread.

1¼ cups milk
1 stick butter
¾ cup sugar
1 teaspoon salt
Dash of nutmeg
2 packages dry yeast
6 cups all-purpose flour
2 eggs and 1 egg yolk
1 cup sugar, mixed with 3 teaspoons cinnamon
2 bread loaf pans

Scald milk, add butter, sugar, salt, and nutmeg, and pour into large mixer bowl. Let cool a little. In another bowl, mix together yeast and 1 cup of the flour and add to milk mixture. Beat for 2 minutes at medium speed with standard mixer blade. Add eggs and beat 3 minutes at medium speed. Slowly add remaining flour and blend well. Change to dough hook and knead 3–4 minutes at medium speed. Put dough in a large buttered bowl, butter top lightly, cover with a damp cloth, and put in an approximately 80-degree oven to rise for 1½–2 hours. Remove from oven and with hands punch down dough. Cover, return to oven, and let rise again for about an hour. Remove from oven and divide dough in two. Shape each half into a rectangle, flatten gently, and spread the top with softened butter, then sprinkle over a generous amount of the sugar-cinnamon mixture (reserving enough for the second loaf and the tops of both). Roll lengthwise, tuck ends underneath, press down seams, and put into buttered bread pan. Repeat for second loaf. Cover the two pans and let rise again in 80-degree oven for abour 45 minutes. Remove from oven, sprinkle remaining sugar-cinnamon mixture over the top of each loaf, and bake in a preheated 350-degree oven for 35 minutes. Bread is baked when tapping the crusty top makes a hollow sound.

LUNCHEON EGG AND ASPARAGUS PIE

6 eggs
⅓ cup light cream
6 tablespoons butter, melted
3 tablespoons flour
Salt and fresh-ground pepper
¾ cup cooked ham, diced
¾ cup Cheddar cheese, grated
15 green asparagus spears (canned)

Beat eggs thoroughly, then add cream, 4 tablespoons of the butter, flour, salt, and pepper. Mix well. Stir in ham and cheese and pour mixture into a buttered 9-inch Pyrex pie pan. Arrange the drained asparagus spears like wheel spokes over the top and drizzle the remaining butter (2 tablespoons) over the asparagus. Bake about 25 minutes in a preheated 325-degree oven (or until set). Remove from oven, cover with foil, and let stand 10 minutes before cutting.

24-HOUR PICKLES

4 long, thin cucumbers
1¼ cups cider vinegar
1½ cups sugar
1 cup water
2 tablespoons salt
1 teaspoon cream of tartar
1 finely sliced onion
½ box pickling spices

Pare cucumbers and cut in quarters the long way. Cut each quarter into 3 or 4 pieces and place in a bowl. In a pan, bring to a boil vinegar, sugar, water, and salt, and pour over cucumbers. Add cream of tartar, onion, and pickling spices and mix well. Store bowl, covered, in refrigerator. They are ready to eat in 24 hours and will keep, in the refrigerator, for about 2 weeks. (Or spoon into sterilized jars and seal.)

QUICHE LORRAINE LINDA

Crust

> 2 cups sifted flour
> 1½ sticks butter, cut into small pieces
> Dash of salt
> 1 egg yolk ⎫
> ¼ cup of water ⎬ lightly beaten together

With fingers, lightly and quickly rub flour and butter together until mixture resembles small peas or coarse bread crumbs. Add salt and egg yolk-water mixture. Blend lightly, roll into a ball, cover with wax paper, and refrigerate for at least 30 minutes (can be overnight). Roll out dough on lightly floured board, fill pie pan (or flan case), prick lightly. Cover crust with aluminum foil wrap. Pour on dried beans to prevent crust from rising during baking, and bake in a preheated 400-degree oven for about 25 minutes. Remove beans and foil and return crust to 350-degree oven for about 5 minutes.

Filling

> 1 whole egg
> 3–4 egg yolks
> ½ pint light cream
> Salt and fresh-ground pepper
> Pinch of cayenne pepper
> Pinch of nutmeg
> 1 medium-sized onion (chopped and sautéed in 2 tablespoons
>   butter)
> ¾ cup diced ham or lightly cooked bacon cut in small pieces
> Chopped chives
> Chopped parsley

Mix together whole egg, yolks, and cream. Season with salt, peppers, and nutmeg. Stir gently. Add onion, ham or bacon, chives, and parsley. Pour into baked piecrust and bake in a 350-degree oven for 15 minutes. Reduce heat to 325 degrees and bake for another 10–15 minutes, until filling is firm but not dry.

HATTIE'S CANDIED GRAPEFRUIT

3 grapefruits (rinds only)
2 cups sugar
1 cup dark brown sugar
⅛ cup water

Cut grapefruit into halves and remove fruit to a separate bowl (or eat it for breakfast). Cut each half rind into four parts. Rinse in cold water, drain, cover with cold water, bring to a boil, and boil for 15 minutes. Repeat this process 4 times. (After the fourth boiling, scrape away some of the pulp to make pieces smooth.) Cut into any shape—bite-sized pieces, diamond-shaped, etc. Rinse once more in cold water, drain, and put in large pan (with lightly oiled bottom). Add sugars and water. Cook mixture, *uncovered,* at high heat, stirring constantly so that it doesn't scorch. Keep scraping the bottom and stirring until sugar is absorbed (20–30 minutes). Pour mixture onto a large platter and with tongs remove pieces to a tray or large cookie tin, covered with wax paper. Do not let them touch each other until they are entirely dry. Turn occasionally, if necessary. Store in an airtight container. Will keep for weeks.

STRAWBERRY JAM

Easy to make and uniquely good. This is an old family recipe and calls for a silver platter. We have never made it without one, but you might take a chance if you can't find a silver platter somewhere in your family. Don't double the recipe

1 pound strawberries
1 pound sugar
1 silver platter

Wash and hull berries. Put in a saucepan with the sugar, bring to a boil, and boil for 14 minutes. Pour onto a silver platter and let stand, uncovered, overnight. Bottle and seal in sterile jars.

NOTE: Some strawberries are juicier than others. If you don't think jam is thick enough, bring it back to a boil for 2–3 minutes in the morning. Then bottle and seal. It probably won't be necessary.

PEACH CANTALOUPE PRESERVE

This is a marvelous preserve but can be best made during two or three weeks in August when both fruits are ripe.

1 heaping quart ripe peeled, diced peaches
1 heaping quart ripe peeled, diced cantaloupes
4 whole lemons, sliced paper thin
6 cups sugar
⅛ teaspoon salt
2 ounces brandy

Put lemons in a saucepan with a cup of water and boil for 10 minutes, then purée them in the blender for 1 minute. Lightly oil bottom of large pan, add peaches, cantaloupe, sugar, and lemon pureé and cook slowly until it boils, stirring constantly. Boil hard for 40–45 minutes (or until thick). Add brandy, and bottle in sterilized jars. Should make about 2 quarts.

BEACH PLUM JELLY

Beach Plum Inn is named after the wild beach plums which grow abundantly only in this area of the Northeast.

2 quarts fully ripened beach plums
2½ cups water
5¾ cups granulated sugar
½ bottle Certo (fruit pectin)
8 8-ounce jelly glasses
2 cakes paraffin wax

Wash plums, which should include some red as well as purple ones. Place in large shallow pan and crush with a mallet. Add the water. Bring to boil, then simmer, covered, 30 minutes. Pour into strainer or jelly bag and allow to strain by gravity only. In this way the best color is maintained.

Measure 3½ cups of the strained juice into a large pot. Add the sugar and mix well. Place over high heat, and while stirring bring to boil. Pour in the fruit pectin. Bring back to boil and boil rapidly for 1 minute. Remove from stove. Skim off foam and pour into sterilized 8-ounce jelly glasses. Cover with about ¼ inch hot liquid paraffin wax. Allow to cool slowly, free from motion, to set wax seal properly. Cover and store. Makes 8 glasses. Will keep indefinitely.

Index

166

The Beach Plum Inn